William Wordsworth
an illustrated selection

The landscape of Wordsworth's boyhood. *Morning on Coniston Fells*, J. M. W. Turner, 1798 (Tate Gallery).

William Wordsworth
an illustrated selection

———

edited with a critical introduction by

JONATHAN WORDSWORTH

The Wordsworth Trust Grasmere

First published 1987 by
The Wordsworth Trust
Dove Cottage, Grasmere, Cumbria LA22 95G

Copyright © The Wordsworth Trust, 1987

British Library Cataloguing in Publication Data
Wordsworth, William *1770–1850*
    [Poems. *Selections*]. William Wordsworth:
    an illustrated selection.
    I. Title   II. Wordsworth, Jonathan
    821′.7   PR5853

    I S B N 0–9510616–5–8

Typeset by Gloucester Typesetting Services
and printed in Great Britain by
Stellar Press, Hatfield, Hertfordshire AL9 7HG

Contents

Preface

This *Selection* follows the pattern of Wordsworth's life, tracing the early years chiefly through episodes from his autobiographical poem, *The Prelude*, and arranging in chronological order poetry written after summer 1797, the beginning of the Great Decade. Texts are from the manuscripts and first printed editions, as prepared for the forthcoming Longman *Annotated Selections*, ed. Jonathan Wordsworth, Nicola Trott and Duncan Wu. Where episodes occur in both the two-part 1799 *Prelude* (abbreviated to *1799*), and the thirteen-book poem of 1805 (*1805*), the earlier text has normally been chosen. Spelling has been modernised, and punctuation is editorial. Excerpts drawn from *The Prelude*, and other longer poems, are given titles as an indication of their content.

Introduction

William Wordsworth was born at Cockermouth on 7 April 1770. The River Derwent ran along the terrace at the bottom of the garden, 'making', as he later put it, 'ceaseless music through the night and day' that 'flowed along my dreams'. It was a very happy start to life; but when he was still only eight his mother died, and the following year he was sent away to school. Here again, though, he was lucky. His landlady, Anne Tyson, was dependable and kind, and Hawkshead Grammar School was set on the banks of Esthwaite Water, among the Cumbrian mountains that were to be so important to his poetry.

Thanks to Wordsworth's great autobiographical poem, *The Prelude*, we know a good deal about his early experiences – furtively borrowing a shepherd's boat, for instance, or joyously skating with friends:

> So through the darkness and the cold we flew,
> And not a voice was idle. With the din,
> Meanwhile, the precipices rang aloud;
> The leafless trees and every icy crag
> Tinkled like iron . . .
> (*Skating on Esthwaite*)

Wordsworth's schooldays seem to have been a blend of happiness and terrors, and as an adult poet he came to value both as essential parts of human experience:

> Fair seed-time had my soul, and I grew up
> Fostered alike by beauty and by fear.
> (*Fair Seed-Time*)

When he was thirteen his father – who was agent to the powerful landowner, Sir James Lowther, later Lord Lonsdale – died suddenly during the Christmas holidays. Wordsworth and his two brothers, 'orphans then, / Followed his body to the grave'. It was an event that he was later to describe in one of the great 'spots of time' of *The Prelude*, but his first attempts to understand bereavement came in *The Vale of Esthwaite*, a clumsy but ambitious poem written when he was only sixteen.

Hawkshead was no ordinary grammar school; under the brilliant young Headmaster, William Taylor (who died in 1786, aged only thirty-two), the boys got an exceptional grounding in maths and classics, and a remarkable proportion went on to successful careers at Cambridge. Wordsworth himself went south to the University in October 1787, and *The Prelude* gives a marvellous account of student life:

> We sauntered, played, we rioted, we talked
> Unprofitable talk at morning hours,
> Drifted about along the streets and walks,
> Read lazily in lazy books, went forth
> To gallop through the country in blind zeal
> Of senseless horsemanship, or on the breast
> Of Cam sailed boisterously, and let the stars
> Come out, perhaps without one quiet thought.
> (*Cambridge Days*)

Looking back, it seemed to have been almost too carefree.

Thanks to the teaching at Hawkshead, Wordsworth arrived at Cambridge a year ahead of his contemporaries in academic terms, but he left in 1792 without an Honours degree. On the other hand, he had read widely (in French and Italian, as well as English), he had written the 450-line *Evening Walk* (published 1793), and in the Long Vacation of 1790 he and a friend had made a tour of France and the Alps. They went on foot, as he later recalled, with twenty pounds between them, and their 'needments tied up in a pocket-handkerchief'. It seems to have been by chance that they landed at Calais on 13 July, but that did not stop them joining the celebrations next day that marked the anniversary of the storming of the Bastille:

> 'Twas a time when Europe was rejoiced,
> France standing on the top of golden hours,
> And human nature seeming born again.
> (*Golden Hours*)

Wordsworth's second visit to France, in 1791–2, proved to be still more important. His family were pressing him to go into the Church, but he was too young to do so, and spent almost a year at Orleans and Blois, learning the language and postponing decisions. At Blois he met a 30 year-old army-officer named Michel Beaupuy, who, despite being himself a member of the nobility, converted him to belief in the Revolution. He also met Annette Vallon, whose child was baptised in Orleans Cathedral as Anne-Caroline Wordsworth on 15 December 1792 – by which time Robespierre had gained the upper hand in Paris, Louis XVI was on trial, and Caroline's father had been forced to return to London. In January 1793 Louis was executed, and in February war was declared between France and England. Two letters survive that show their relationship to have been a tender one, but it was ten years before Wordsworth and Annette were able to meet again, during the Peace of Amiens (1802). The poet had no job and no money, and his family would not have approved, but had the war ended quickly, they would surely have got married. As it was, they grew apart.

It was Wordsworth's sister Dorothy whose companionship came to represent for him both stability and inspiration. They had been separated as children after their mother's death, but it seems that from an early age they had planned to set up house together. In spring 1794 they were able to spend six happy and productive weeks at Windy Brow, near Keswick, and in autumn of the following year they were lent a farmhouse at Racedown in Dorset. They were poor, but a consumptive friend, named Raisley Calvert, had left Wordsworth £900 as an act of faith in his ability as a writer, and they lived very frugally on the income. The poetry of 1793–6 – *Salisbury Plain* in its two versions, and Wordsworth's only play, *The Borderers* – was concerned chiefly with social comment and political philosophy. For a time the poet became a follower of William Godwin, whose *Political Justice* (1793) proclaimed that human reason would finally lead to a just and egalitarian society. He could not, however, be satisfied with Godwin for very long. His shrewdness told him that reason could be put to bad ends as well as good, and his deepest intuitions told him that love, emotion, imagination – all of them outlawed by Godwin – were to him vitally important.

To judge from *The Prelude*, there was a moment in the spring of 1796 when this conflict led to a form of nervous breakdown, in which the poet,

> Sick, wearied out with contrarieties,
> Yielded up moral questions in despair ...
> (*Confusion and Recovery*)

Dorothy, however, was at hand, and her reassurance, coupled with the beauty of the Dorset countryside, restored his confidence in himself and in his calling as a writer.

The Great Decade, in which Wordsworth wrote almost all his best-loved poetry, spans the years 1797–1806 – from *The Ruined Cottage* to *Elegiac Stanzas*. In summer 1797, when *The Ruined Cottage* was written, he and Dorothy were still in Dorset. The poem is a beautiful and tragic account of a woman whose husband can get no work because of the war, is forced to enlist, and never returns. Just as the first draft was completed, Coleridge arrived on a visit to Racedown. It is an immensely important moment. On 6 June, Dorothy writes to her schoolfriend, Mary Hutchinson (the poet's future wife):

You had a great loss in not seeing Coleridge. He is a wonderful man. His conversation teems with soul, mind, and spirit. . . . The first thing that was read after he came was William's new poem, *The Ruined Cottage*, with which he was much delighted; and after

4

tea he repeated to us two acts and a half of his tragedy, *Osorio*. The next morning William read his tragedy, *The Borderers* . . .

At once the pattern is set up that is to produce the greatest work in both writers – a sharing of their poetry and ideas in close personal companionship.

Within a month, Wordsworth and Dorothy had moved to Alfoxden in Somerset to be near Coleridge in the neighbouring village of Nether Stowey. By the end of the year, Coleridge had not only finished *Osorio* (and composed the important conversation poem, *This Lime Tree Bower My Prison*), but also written *Kubla Khan* and a first version of his great ballad, *The Ancient Mariner*. Wordsworth, meanwhile, was not so much writing, as listening and thinking. When he does again start to compose, in February 1798, we hear a new voice – the voice of a poet who can tell us of the workings of the human mind, of visionary moods, and sources of inward strength:

> Thus did I steal along that silent road,
> My body from the stillness drinking in
> A restoration like the calm of sleep
> But sweeter far. . . .
>   What beauteous pictures now
> Rose in harmonious imagery! They rose
> As from some distant region of my soul
> And came along like dreams . . .
>   (*The Discharged Soldier*)

The influence of Coleridge is impossible to define, but is felt now in everything that Wordsworth writes – above all in his portrayal of the One Life, the force within the natural world which may be sensed as love, or joy, but which is truly the presence of God. Sometimes his tones are lyrical:

> Love now, an universal birth,
> From heart to heart is stealing –
> From earth to man, from man to earth –
> It is the hour of feeling!
>   (*To My Sister*)

Sometimes they have a grandeur that only Milton can match:

> that serene and blessed mood
> In which the affections gently lead us on,
> Until, the breath of this corporeal frame
> And even the motion of our human blood
> Almost suspended, we are laid asleep
> In body and become a living soul,
> While, with an eye made quiet by the power
> Of harmony and the deep power of joy,
> We see into the life of things.
>
> (*Tintern Abbey*)

By the autumn of 1798 the poet and Dorothy were at Goslar in Germany, where, in the coldest winter of the century, Wordsworth's thoughts went back to his childhood. Very rapidly he drafted a series of episodes that proved to be the beginnings of *The Prelude*. And he found time as well to write the strange and haunting Lucy Poems:

> She shall be sportive as the fawn
> That wild with glee across the lawn
> Or up the mountain springs;
> And hers shall be the breathing balm,
> And hers the silence and the calm,
> Of mute insensate things.
>
> (*Three Years She Grew*)

Before they left Germany in February 1799, Wordsworth had completed the first half of the original two-part *Prelude*, covering the childhood experiences that were so vital to his imaginative life. By the end of the year, Part Two, covering adolescence, was also complete. Then, in the last days of the eighteenth century, the poet and his sister moved into Dove Cottage, the small but strongly-built house in Grasmere that had once been an inn – the Dove and Olive Bough.

Wordsworth at this stage had published very little – since *An Evening Walk* and *Descriptive Sketches* in 1793, only the anonymous *Lyrical Ballads* of 1798 – and though we can see now that he was the greatest living poet, he was virtually unknown. He hated publication, and was engaged on a massive long-term project, *The Recluse*, in which the verse that he was storing up (including *The Prelude*) was going to be incorporated. Delighted that he and Dorothy now had a house of their own, he began work on the central philosophical section of *The Recluse* by writing *Home at Grasmere*. Though striving to offer a larger perspective, the poem is above all a thanksgiving for the poet's tender, contented, loving relationship with his sister:

> Where'er my footsteps turned,
> Her voice was like a hidden bird that sang;
> The thought of her was like a flash of light
> Or an unseen companionship, a breath
> Or fragrance independent of the wind . . .
> (*Tribute to Dorothy*)

The end of 1800 saw the writing of *Michael* and also the republication of *Lyrical Ballads*, now in two volumes, and with Wordsworth's name on the title-page. Included for the first time was the Preface, which, as well as being famous for its theory of 'emotion recollected in tranquility', was in Coleridge's view responsible for the critics' hostility to Wordsworth over the next twenty years.

Life at Dove Cottage was busy and delightful. Its details live again in the vivid prose of Dorothy's *Journal*:

Sunday 12th October. Beautiful day. Sat in the house writing in the morning while William went into the wood to compose . . . copied poems for the *Lyrical Ballads*. . . . We pulled apples after dinner, a large basket full. We walked before tea by Bainriggs to observe the many-coloured foliage, the oaks dark green with yellow leaves; the birches generally still green, some near the water yellowish; the sycamore crimson and crimson-tufted . . .

Wordsworth composed chiefly out of doors, and worked in bursts of inspired creativity: almost nothing in 1801 and 1803, thousands of lines of great poetry in 1800 and

1802 and 1804–5. The poems of spring 1802, addressed to birds, flowers, butterflies, and celebrating light-heartedly the beauties of Nature, have an atmosphere all their own. There are moments of greater seriousness – the opening stanzas of the *Ode*, for instance (completed 1804), and *The Leech-Gatherer* – but the prevailing mood, until the great Miltonic sonnets of the summer, is one of tender playfulness:

> Oh pleasant, pleasant were the days,
> The time when in our childish plays
> My sister Emmeline and I
> Together chased the butterfly.
> A very hunter, I did rush
> Upon the prey – with leaps and springs
> I followed on from brake to bush –
> But she, God love her, feared to brush
> The dust from off its wings!
>
> (*To a Butterfly*)

Perhaps we should see in this nostalgia a sense of impending change, of outside events pressing in upon the world of Dove Cottage. In the summer of 1802 the Peace of Amiens made it possible for Wordsworth and Dorothy to cross to France. Other British tourists went at this moment to see the treasures amassed by Napoleon in the Louvre; Dorothy and William went instead to spend a month with Annette (whom Wordsworth had not seen since 1792) and Caroline, who was nine, but who had never met her father. Dorothy did not keep her *Journal*, and though Wordsworth wrote one beautiful sonnet for Caroline, we know little of his feelings or Annette's. Part of the reason for his visit, however, was that he was going to be married to Mary Hutchinson in October.

Though she may never have permitted herself to think in such terms, Dorothy was as likely to be put out as Annette. Mary was an old friend, and had stayed with them for long periods at both Racedown and Dove Cottage. No one could have been less threatening, or moved

The road outside Dove Cottage. T. M. Richardson, 1784–1828
(Wordsworth Trust).

Dove Cottage in the 1820s. Dora Wordsworth after Amos Green
(Wordsworth Trust).

in with less disturbance of their cherished way of life, but William would from now on have to be shared – and shared with a wife. In the event, we see Dorothy losing her role as special companion to her brother, and becoming, contentedly, a second mother to the children. The inspiration of her writing, however, persists. If anything is more compelling than Wordsworth's famous *Daffodils* of 1804, it is Dorothy's prose description (15 April 1802) which he took as his source:

I never saw daffodils so beautiful; they grew among the mossy stones, about and about them. Some rested their heads upon these stones as upon a pillow for weariness, and the rest tossed and reeled and danced, and seemed as if they verily laughed with the wind that blew upon them over the lake, they looked so gay, ever glancing, ever changing.

The spring of 1804 was memorable for Coleridge's departure for the Mediterranean. He had been living since July 1800 at Keswick, twelve miles from Grasmere, writing a few sad, impressive poems – notably *Dejection* and *Pains of Sleep* – but mainly reading his way into German philosophy. His marriage was wretched, and opium had undermined his health; his friends at Dove Cottage feared he was dying. Wordsworth's response was to move into what was probably the most creative period of his life. A five-book version of *The Prelude* was made for Coleridge to take with him, and then scrapped in March when it was almost complete. Meanwhile Dorothy and Mary were compiling a volume of the shorter unpublished poems as a gift to Coleridge, and Wordsworth himself found time to complete the *Ode* (begun in 1802), as well as writing *Daffodils* and *Ode to Duty*.

Nor did the activity cease when Coleridge sailed: Wordsworth forged straight ahead with *The Prelude*, finishing the poem in thirteen books in May 1805. It turned out, as he told Sir George Beaumont in a letter, to be a sad day. The poet's brother John, to whom they all felt especially close, and who (though only 33) was commander of the largest ship in the East India fleet, had been drowned in February off the Dorset coast. Wordsworth tried again and again to write the appropriate elegy, and when he succeeded, more than a year later, it seemed that he was saying farewell also to an earlier self:

> I have submitted to a new control –
> A power is gone, which nothing can restore –
> A deep distress hath humanised my soul.
> (*Elegiac Stanzas*)

The greatest poetry had all been written. It was the work of a young man, and Wordsworth now was approaching middle age. At the height of his powers in 1804 he had written, 'I long for a repose which ever is the same' (*Ode to Duty*), and at some level he was tired of his 'vexing' creativity. In 1808 the family had to move out of Dove Cottage, which had become too small for them; but they continued to live in Grasmere, first at Allan Bank, and then at the old Rectory. In 1812 two of the poet's five children, Catharine and Thomas, died, and when next year the household moved to Rydal Mount (two miles along the road to Ambleside), it was partly to escape the sad proximity of their graves, seen through the Rectory windows. Shortly before the move to Rydal, Wordsworth became a civil servant, obtaining through the new Lord Lonsdale the job of Distributor of Stamps for Westmorland. In 1814 he published *The Excursion*, in a large and handsome quarto volume – one of the last of its kind.

Like *The Prelude*, *The Excursion* was intended to be a part of *The Recluse*; the difference was that the poet felt he couldn't justify publishing his autobiography until the project as a whole was complete. As a result, *The Prelude* remained in manuscript for forty-five years – two generations. Save for a small circle (including notably Coleridge and De Quincey), Wordsworth's contemporaries were unaware of his greatest poem. His reputation had to depend upon *The Excursion*, which though it produced some fine things – *Cloudscape New Jerusalem* and *Two-Fold Image* among them – was on the whole solemn, and less imaginative. Reviewers in 1814 were still fighting a vendetta against the Preface to *Lyrical Ballads*, but gradually Wordsworth came to be recognised as the outstanding poet of his age. He never ceased to write, and though the work of his middle and later years tends to lack the strength and originality of the Great Decade, there were always the unexpected moments that took him back into his former self – *Surprised by Joy*, for instance, on the death of little Catharine, the Duddon *Conclusion*, and *Airey-Force Valley*:

> even now, a little breeze (perchance
> Escaped from boisterous winds that rage without)
> Has entered, by the sturdy oaks unfelt –
> But to its gentle touch how sensitive
> Is the light ash, that, pendent from the brow
> Of yon dim cave, in seeming silence makes
> A soft eye-music of slow-waving boughs . . .

Last, and saddest, of these works that catch again the early power is the *Extempore Effusion*, written when the poet was sixty-five. Nominally about the death of his Scottish contemporary, James Hogg, the poem is above all a leave-taking for Coleridge and Lamb, who had died the previous year (1834):

> Nor has the rolling year twice measured,
> From sign to sign, its steadfast course,
> Since every mortal power of Coleridge
> Was frozen at its marvellous source –
>
> The rapt one, of the godlike forehead,
> The heaven-eyed creature sleeps in earth;
> And Lamb, the frolic and the gentle,
> Has vanished from his lonely hearth.

> Like clouds that rake the mountain-summits,
> Or waves that own no curbing hand,
> How fast has brother followed brother
> From sunshine to the sunless land!

Wordsworth himself died in 1850, on 23 April – St George's Day, and by chance also the anniversary of Shakespeare's death. He was eighty. Since 1843 he had been Poet Laureate, and his public image in the later years was not one that would have been predicted by the revolutionary of the 1790s. In many ways, however, he was true to himself and his early ideals. His poetry speaks of a timeless world, as relevant now as when it was written. As Matthew Arnold put it, in his famous *Memorial Verses*:

> He found us when the age had bound
> Our souls in its benumbing round;
> He spoke, and loosed our heart in tears.
> He laid us as we lay at birth
> On the cool, flowery lap of earth . . .
> The hills were round us, and the breeze
> Went o'er the sun-lit fields again . . .

William Wordsworth
an illustrated selection

Fair Seed-Time

Oh, many a time have I, a five years' child,
A naked boy, in one delightful rill,
A little mill-race severed from his stream,
Made one long bathing of a summer's day,
Basked in the sun, and plunged, and basked again,
Alternate, all a summer's day, or coursed
Over the sandy fields, leaping through groves
Of yellow grunsel; or – when crag and hill,
The woods, and distant Skiddaw's lofty height,
Were bronzed with a deep radiance – stood alone
Beneath the sky, as if I had been born
On Indian plains, and from my mother's hut
Had run abroad in wantonness to sport,
A naked savage, in the thunder-shower.
    Fair seed-time had my soul, and I grew up
Fostered alike by beauty and by fear . . .

(*1805* i, 291–306)

The Shepherd and His Dog

I remember, far from home
Once having strayed while yet a very child,
I saw a sight – and with what joy and love!
It was a day of exhalations spread
Upon the mountains, mists and steam-like fogs
Rebounding everywhere, not vehement
But calm and mild, gentle and beautiful,
With gleams of sunshine on the eyelet spots
And loopholes of the hills – wherever seen,
Hidden by quiet process, and as soon
Unfolded, to be huddled up again.
   Along a narrow valley and profound
I journeyed, when aloft above my head,
Emerging from the silvery vapours, lo,
A shepherd and his dog, in open day!
Girt round with mists they stood, and looked about
From that enclosure small, inhabitants
Of an aerial island floating on,
As seemed, with that abode in which they were,
A little pendant area of grey rocks,
By the soft wind breathed forward.

(*1805* viii, 81–101)

There Was a Boy

There was a boy – ye knew him well, ye cliffs
And islands of Winander. Many a time
At evening, when the stars had just begun
To move along the edges of the hills,
Rising or setting, would he stand alone
Beneath the trees or by the glimmering lake,
And there, with fingers interwoven, both hands
Pressed closely palm to palm, and to his mouth
Uplifted, he as through an instrument
Blew mimic hootings to the silent owls
That they might answer him. And they would shout
Across the watery vale, and shout again,
Responsive to his call, with quivering peals
And long halloos, and screams, and echoes loud,
Redoubled and redoubled – concourse wild
Of mirth and jocund din.
                                And when it chanced
That pauses of deep silence mocked his skill,
Then sometimes in that silence, while he hung
Listening, a gentle shock of mild surprise
Has carried far into his heart the voice
Of mountain torrents; or the visible scene
Would enter unawares into his mind
With all its solemn imagery, its rocks,
Its woods, and that uncertain heaven, received
Into the bosom of the steady lake.

(*1805* v, 389–413)

Skating on Esthwaite Water

And in the frosty season, when the sun
Was set, and visible for many a mile
The cottage windows through the twilight blazed,
I heeded not the summons. Clear and loud
The village-clock tolled six; I wheeled about
Proud and exulting, like an untired horse
That cares not for its home.
                                    All shod with steel
We hissed along the polished ice in games
Confederate, imitative of the chase
And woodland pleasures, the resounding horn,
The pack loud bellowing, and the hunted hare.
So through the darkness and the cold we flew,
And not a voice was idle. With the din,
Meanwhile, the precipices rang aloud;
The leafless trees and every icy crag
Tinkled like iron; while the distant hills
Into the tumult sent an alien sound
Of melancholy, not unnoticed; while the stars,
Eastward, were sparkling clear, and in the west
The orange sky of evening died away.
    Not seldom from the uproar I retired
Into a silent bay, or sportively
Glanced sideway, leaving the tumultuous throng,
To cut across the shadow of a star
That gleamed upon the ice. And oftentimes
When we had given our bodies to the wind
And all the shadowy banks on either side
Came sweeping through the darkness, spinning still
The rapid line of motion, then at once
Have I, reclining back upon my heels,
Stopped short – yet still the solitary cliffs
Wheeled by me, even as if the earth had rolled
With visible motion her diurnal round.

Behind me did they stretch in solemn train,
Feebler and feebler, and I stood and watched
Till all was tranquil as a summer sea.

(*1799* i, 150–185)

                          'Twas my joy
To wander half the night among the cliffs
And the smooth hollows where the woodcocks ran
Along the moonlight turf. In thought and wish
That time, my shoulder all with springes hung,
I was a fell destroyer. Gentle powers,
Who give us happiness and call it peace,
When scudding on from snare to snare I plied
My anxious visitation, hurrying on,
Still hurrying, hurrying onward, how my heart
Panted! – among the scattered yew-trees and the crags
That looked upon me, how my bosom beat
With expectation! Sometimes strong desire
Resistless overpowered me, and the bird
Which was the captive of another's toils
Became my prey; and when the deed was done
I heard among the solitary hills
Low breathings coming after me, and sounds
Of undistinguishable motion, steps
Almost as silent as the turf they trod.
    Nor less in springtime, when on southern banks
The shining sun had from his knot of leaves
Decoyed the primrose flower, and when the vales
And woods were warm, was I a rover then
In the high places, on the lonesome peaks,
Among the mountains and the winds. Though mean
And though inglorious were my views, the end
Was not ignoble. Oh, when I have hung
Above the raven's nest, by knots of grass
Or half-inch fissures in the slippery rock
But ill sustained, and almost, as it seemed,
Suspended by the blast which blew amain,
Shouldering the naked crag, oh, at that time,
While on the perilous ridge I hung alone,

With what strange utterance did the loud dry wind
Blow through my ears; the sky seemed not a sky
Of earth, and with what motion moved the clouds!
  The mind of man is fashioned and built up
Even as a strain of music. I believe
That there are spirits which, when they would form
A favoured being, from his very dawn
Of infancy do open out the clouds
As at the touch of lightning, seeking him
With gentle visitation – quiet powers,
Retired, and seldom recognised, yet kind,
And to the very meanest not unknown –
With me, though rarely, in my boyish days
They communed. Others too there are, who use,
Yet haply aiming at the self-same end,
Severer interventions, ministry
More palpable – and of their school was I.
  They guided me: one evening led by them
I went alone into a shepherd's boat,
A skiff, that to a willow-tree was tied
Within a rocky cave, its usual home.
The moon was up, the lake was shining clear
Among the hoary mountains; from the shore
I pushed, and struck the oars, and struck again
In cadence, and my little boat moved on
Just like a man who walks with stately step
Though bent on speed. It was an act of stealth
And troubled pleasure. Not without the voice
Of mountain-echoes did my boat move on,
Leaving behind her still on either side
Small circles glittering idly in the moon,
Until they melted all into one track
Of sparkling light.
                    A rocky steep uprose
Above the cavern of the willow-tree,
And now, as suited one who proudly rowed
With his best skill, I fixed a steady view

Upon the top of that same craggy ridge,
The bound of the horizon – for behind
Was nothing but the stars and the grey sky.
She was an elfin pinnace; twenty times
I dipped my oars into the silent lake,
And as I rose upon the stroke my boat
Went heaving through the water like a swan –
When from behind that rocky steep, till then
The bound of the horizon, a huge cliff,
As if with voluntary power instinct,
Upreared its head. I struck, and struck again,
And, growing still in stature, the huge cliff
Rose up between me and the stars, and still,
With measured motion, like a living thing
Strode after me.
             With trembling hands I turned,
And through the silent water stole my way
Back to the cavern of the willow-tree.
There in her mooring-place I left my bark,
And through the meadows homeward went with grave
And serious thoughts; and after I had seen
That spectacle, for many days my brain
Worked with a dim and undetermined sense
Of unknown modes of being. In my thoughts
There was a darkness – call it solitude,
Or blank desertion – no familiar shapes
Of hourly objects, images of trees,
Of sea or sky, no colours of green fields,
But huge and mighty forms that do not live
Like living men moved slowly through my mind
By day, and were the trouble of my dreams.

(*1799* i, 30–129)

Spots of Time

                        In the very week
When I was first transplanted to thy vale,
Beloved Hawkshead – when thy paths, thy shores
And brooks, were like a dream of novelty
To my half-infant mind – I chanced to cross
One of those open fields which, shaped like ears,
Make green peninsulas on Esthwaite's lake.
Twilight was coming on, yet through the gloom
I saw distinctly on the opposite shore,
Beneath a tree and close by the lake side,
A heap of garments, as if left by one
Who there was bathing. Half an hour I watched
And no one owned them; meanwhile the calm lake
Grew dark with all the shadows on its breast,
And now and then a leaping fish disturbed
The breathless stillness. The succeeding day
There came a company, and in their boat
Sounded with iron hooks and with long poles.
At length the dead man, mid that beauteous scene
Of trees and hills and water, bolt upright
Rose with his ghastly face . . .
    There are in our existence spots of time
Which with distinct preeminence retain
A fructifying virtue, whence, depressed
By trivial occupations and the round
Of ordinary intercourse, our minds –
Especially the imaginative power –
Are nourished and invisibly repaired.
Such moments chiefly seem to have their date
In our first childhood.
                        I remember well
('Tis of an early season that I speak,
The twilight of rememberable life),
While I was yet an urchin, one who scarce

Could hold a bridle, with ambitious hopes
I mounted, and we rode towards the hills.
We were a pair of horsemen: honest James
Was with me, my encourager and guide.
We had not travelled long ere some mischance
Disjoined me from my comrade, and, through fear
Dismounting, down the rough and stony moor
I led my horse, and, stumbling on, at length
Came to a bottom where in former times
A man, the murderer of his wife, was hung
In irons. Mouldered was the gibbet-mast;
The bones were gone, the iron and the wood;
Only a long green ridge of turf remained
Whose shape was like a grave.
                                        I left the spot,
And reascending the bare slope I saw
A naked pool that lay beneath the hills,
The beacon on the summit, and more near
A girl who bore a pitcher on her head
And seemed with difficult steps to force her way
Against the blowing wind. It was in truth
An ordinary sight, but I should need
Colours and words that are unknown to man
To paint the visionary dreariness
Which, while I looked all round for my lost guide,
Did at that time invest the naked pool,
The beacon on the lonely eminence,
The woman and her garments vexed and tossed
By the strong wind.
                                Nor less I recollect
(Long after, though my childhood had not ceased)
Another scene which left a kindred power
Implanted in my mind. One Christmas-time,
The day before the holidays began,
Feverish, and tired, and restless, I went forth
Into the fields, impatient for the sight
Of those three horses which should bear us home,

Sole light admitted here, a small cascade,
Illumes with sparkling foam the twilight shade.

Lower Fall at Rydal, Joseph Farington, 1787 (Jonathan
Wordsworth).

My brothers and myself. There was a crag,
An eminence, which from the meeting-point
Of two highways ascending overlooked
At least a long half-mile of those two roads,
By each of which the expected steeds might come –
The choice uncertain. Thither I repaired
Up to the highest summit. 'Twas a day
Stormy, and rough, and wild, and on the grass
I sat half sheltered by a naked wall.
Upon my right hand was a single sheep,
A whistling hawthorn on my left, and there,
Those two companions at my side, I watched
With eyes intensely straining, as the mist
Gave intermitting prospects of the wood
And plain beneath.

               Ere I to school returned
That dreary time, ere I had been ten days
A dweller in my father's house, he died,
And I and my two brothers, orphans then,
Followed his body to the grave. The event,
With all the sorrow which it brought, appeared
A chastisement; and when I called to mind
That day so lately passed, when from the crag
I looked in such anxiety of hope,
With trite reflections of morality,
Yet with the deepest passion, I bowed low
To God who thus corrected my desires.

And afterwards the wind and sleety rain,
And all the business of the elements,
The single sheep, and the one blasted tree,
And the bleak music of that old stone wall,
The noise of wood and water, and the mist
Which on the line of each of those two roads
Advanced in such indisputable shapes –
All these were spectacles and sounds to which
I often would repair, and thence would drink

As at a fountain. And I do not doubt
That in this later time, when storm and rain
Beat on my roof at midnight, or by day
When I am in the woods, unknown to me
The workings of my spirit thence are brought.

(*1799* i, 259–79, 288–374)

Wisdom and Spirit of the Universe

Wisdom and spirit of the universe –
Thou soul that art the eternity of thought,
That givest to forms and images a breath
And everlasting motion – not in vain,
By day or star-light, thus from my first dawn
Of childhood didst thou intertwine for me
The passions that build up our human soul
Not with the mean and vulgar works of man,
But with high objects, with enduring things,
With life and Nature, purifying thus
The elements of feeling and of thought,
And sanctifying by such discipline
Both pain and fear, until we recognise
A grandeur in the beatings of the heart.

(*1805* i, 428–41)

Furness Abbey

Nor is my aim neglected if I tell
How twice in the long length of those half-years
We from our funds perhaps with bolder hand
Drew largely, anxious for one day at least
To feel the motion of the galloping steed;
And with the good old innkeeper, in truth
I needs must say, that sometimes we have used
Sly subterfuge, for the intended bound
Of the day's journey was too distant far
For any cautious man: a structure famed
Beyond its neighbourhood, the antique walls
Of a large abbey, with its fractured arch,
Belfry, and images, and living trees –
A holy scene. Along the smooth green turf
Our horses grazed. In more than inland peace
Left by the winds that overpass the vale,
In that sequestered ruin trees and towers
(Both silent and both motionless alike)
Hear all day long the murmuring sea that beats
Incessantly upon a craggy shore.
  Our steeds remounted, and the summons given,
With whip and spur we by the chantry flew
In uncouth race, and left the cross-legged knight
And the stone abbot, and that single wren
Which one day sang so sweetly in the nave
Of the old church that, though from recent showers
The earth was comfortless, and, touched by faint
Internal breezes, from the roofless walls
The shuddering ivy dripped large drops, yet still
So sweetly mid the gloom the invisible bird
Sang to itself that there I could have made
My dwelling-place, and lived for ever there,
To hear such music.
                    Through the walls we flew

        the antique walls
Of a large abbey, with its fractured arch,
Belfry, and images, and living trees –
A holy scene. Along the smooth green turf
Our horses grazed . . .

Furness Abbey, Thomas Hearne, 1777, engraved T. Medland
1782.

And down the valley, and, a circuit made
In wantonness of heart, through rough and smooth
We scampered homeward. O, ye rocks and streams,
And that still spirit of the evening air,
Even in this joyous time I sometimes felt
Your presence, when, with slackened step, we breathed
Along the sides of the steep hills, or when,
Lightened by gleams of moonlight from the sea,
We beat with thundering hoofs the level sand.

(*1799* ii, 98–139)

'The minstrel of our troop'. Paul Sandby, 1730–1809 (Jonathan Wordsworth).

The Minstrel of the Troop

                    But ere the fall
Of night, when in our pinnace we returned
Over the dusky lake, and to the beach
Of some small island steered our course, with one,
The minstrel of our troop, and left him there,
And rowed off gently while he blew his flute
Alone upon the rock, oh, then the calm
And dead still water lay upon my mind
Even with a weight of pleasure, and the sky,
Never before so beautiful, sank down
Into my heart and held me like a dream.

                    (*1799* ii, 204–14)

An Auxiliar Light

                    A plastic power
Abode with me, a forming hand, at times
Rebellious, acting in a devious mood –
A local spirit of its own, at war
With general tendency – but for the most
Subservient strictly to the external things
With which it communed. An auxiliar light
Came from my mind, which on the setting sun
Bestowed new splendour; the melodious birds,
The gentle breezes, fountains that ran on
Murmuring so sweetly in themselves, obeyed
A like dominion, and the midnight storm
Grew darker in the presence of my eye.
Hence my obeisance, my devotion hence,
And hence my transport.

                              (*1799* ii, 411–25)

Cambridge Days

                          Companionships,
Friendships, acquaintances, were welcome all;
We sauntered, played, we rioted, we talked
Unprofitable talk at morning hours,
Drifted about along the streets and walks,
Read lazily in lazy books, went forth
To gallop through the country in blind zeal
Of senseless horsemanship, or on the breast
Of Cam sailed boisterously, and let the stars
Come out, perhaps without one quiet thought.

                         (*1805* iii, 249–58)

The Lower Fall at Rydal

Then Quiet led me up the huddling rill,
Brightening with water-breaks the sombrous gill,
To where, while thick above the branches close,
In dark-brown basin its wild waves repose;
Inverted shrubs and moss of darkest green
Cling from the rocks, with pale wood-weeds between –
Save that, atop, the subtle sunbeams shine
On withered briars that o'er the crags recline;
Sole light admitted here, a small cascade,
Illumes with sparkling foam the twilight shade.
Beyond, along the vista of the brook,
Where antique roots its bustling path o'erlook,
The eye reposes on a secret bridge
Half grey, half shagged with ivy to its ridge.

(1789 *Evening Walk*, 71–84)

The Discharged Soldier

                              I love to walk
Along the public way when, for the night
Deserted in its silence, it assumes
A character of deeper quietness
Than pathless solitudes. At such a time
I slowly mounted up a steep ascent
Where the road's watery surface to the ridge
Of that sharp rising glittered in the moon,
And seemed before my eyes another stream
Stealing with silent lapse to join the brook
That murmured in the valley. On I passed
Tranquil – receiving in my own despite
Amusement, as I slowly passed along,
From such near objects as from time to time
Perforce disturbed the slumber of the sense
Quiescent and disposed to sympathy –
With an exhausted mind worn out by toil
And all unworthy of the deeper joy
Which waits on distant prospect, cliff or sea,
The dark blue vault, and universe of stars.
    Thus did I steal along that silent road,
My body from the stillness drinking in
A restoration like the calm of sleep
But sweeter far. Above, before, behind,
Around me, all was peace and solitude:
I looked not round, nor did the solitude
Speak to my eye, but it was heard and felt.
Oh happy state! What beauteous pictures now
Rose in harmonious imagery! They rose
As from some distant region of my soul
And came along like dreams – yet such as left
Obscurely mingled with their passing forms
A consciousness of animal delight,
A self-possession felt in every pause

And every gentle movement of my frame.
  While thus I wandered, step by step led on,
It chanced a sudden turning of the road
Presented to my view an uncouth shape
So near that, stepping back into the shade
Of a thick hawthorn, I could mark him well,
Myself unseen. He was in stature tall,
A foot above man's common measure tall,
And lank, and upright. There was in his form
A meagre stiffness – you might almost think
That his bones wounded him. His legs were long,
So long and shapeless that I looked at them
Forgetful of the body they sustained.
His arms were long and lean; his hands were bare;
His visage, wasted though it seemed, was large
In feature; his cheeks sunken; and his mouth
Showed ghastly in the moonlight. From behind,
A milestone propped him, and his figure seemed
Half sitting and half standing. I could mark
That he was clad in military garb,
Though faded yet entire.
                        His face was turned
Towards the road, yet not as if he sought
For any living thing. He appeared
Forlorn and desolate, a man cut off
From all his kind, and more than half detached
From his own nature. He was alone,
Had no attendant, neither dog, nor staff,
Nor knapsack – in his very dress appeared
A desolation, a simplicity,
That appertained to solitude. I think
If but a glove had dangled in his hand
It would have made him more akin to man.
Long time I scanned him with a mingled sense
Of fear and sorrow. From his lips meanwhile
There issued murmuring sounds as if of pain
Or of uneasy thought; yet still his form

Kept the same fearful steadiness. His shadow
Lay at his feet and moved not.
                              In a glen
Hard by, a village stood, whose silent doors
Were visible among the scattered trees,
Scarce distant from the spot an arrow's flight.
I wished to see him move, but he remained
Fixed to his place, and still from time to time
Sent forth a murmuring voice of dead complaint,
A groan scarce audible. Yet all the while
The chained mastiff in his wooden house
Was vexed, and from among the village-trees
Howled never ceasing.
                        Not without reproach
Had I prolonged my watch, and now confirmed,
And my heart's specious cowardice subdued,
I left the shady nook where I had stood
And hailed the stranger. From his resting-place
He rose, and, with his lean and wasted arm
In measured gesture lifted to his head,
Returned my salutation. A short while
I held discourse on things indifferent
And casual matter. He meanwhile had ceased
From all complaint – his station had resumed,
Propped by the milestone as before. And when erelong
I asked his history, he in reply
Was neither slow nor eager, but unmoved,
And with a quiet uncomplaining voice,
A stately air of mild indifference,
He told a simple fact: that he had been
A soldier, to the Tropic Isles had gone,
Whence he had landed now some ten days past;
That on his landing he had been dismissed,
And with the little strength he yet had left
Was travelling to regain his native home.
   At this I turned, and through the trees looked down
Into the village – all were gone to rest,

Nor smoke nor any taper-light appeared,
But every silent window to the moon
Shone with a yellow glitter. 'No one there',
Said I, 'is waking. We must measure back
The way which we have come. Behind yon wood
A labourer dwells, an honest man and kind;
He will not murmur should we break his rest,
And he will give you food if food you need,
And lodging for the night.' At this he stooped,
And from the ground took up an oaken staff
By me yet unobserved, a traveller's staff,
Which I suppose from his slack hand had dropped,
And (such the langour of the weary man)
Had lain till now neglected in the grass,
But not forgotten. Back we turned and shaped
Our course toward the cottage. He appeared
To travel without pain, and I beheld
With ill-suppressed astonishment his tall
And ghostly figure moving at my side.

 As we advanced I asked him for what cause
He tarried there, nor had demanded rest
At inn or cottage. He replied, 'In truth
My weakness made me loth to move, and here
I felt myself at ease and much relieved –
But that the village-mastiff fretted me,
And every second moment rang a peal
Felt at my very heart. There was no noise,
Nor any foot abroad; I do not know
What ailed him, but it seemed as if the dog
Were howling to the murmur of the stream.'

 While thus we travelled on I did not fail
To question him of what he had endured
From war and battle and the pestilence.
He all the while was in demeanour calm,
Concise in answer: solemn and sublime
He might have seemed, but that in all he said
There was a strange half-absence and a tone

Of weakness and indifference, as of one
Remembering the importance of his theme,
But feeling it no longer. We advanced
Slowly, and ere we to the wood were come
Discourse had ceased.
                    Together on we passed
In silence through the shades gloomy and dark,
Then turning up along an open field
We gained the cottage. At the door I knocked,
And called aloud, 'My friend, here is a man
By sickness overcome; beneath your roof
This night let him find rest, and give him food –
The service if need be I will requite.'
Assured that now my comrade would repose
In comfort, I entreated that henceforth
He would not linger in the public ways
But at the door of cottage or of inn
Demand the succour which his state required,
And told him, feeble as he was, 'twere fit
He asked relief or alms. At this reproof,
With the same ghastly mildness in his look,
He said, 'My trust is in the God of Heaven,
And in the eye of him that passes me.'

   By this the labourer had unlocked the door,
And now my comrade touched his hat again
With his lean hand, and, in a voice that seemed
To speak with a reviving interest
Till then unfelt, he thanked me. I returned
The blessing of the poor unhappy man,
And so we parted.

Vows were then Made for Me

                              I had passed
The night in dancing, gaiety and mirth –
With din of instruments, and shuffling feet,
And glancing forms, and tapers glittering,
And unaimed prattle flying up and down,
Spirits upon the stretch, and here and there
Slight shocks of young love-liking interspersed
That mounted up like joy into the head,
And tingled through the veins. Ere we retired
The cock had crowed, the sky was bright with day;
Two miles I had to walk along the fields
Before I reached my home.
                              Magnificent
The morning was, a memorable pomp,
More glorious than I ever had beheld.
The sea was laughing at a distance; all
The solid mountains were as bright as clouds,
Grain-tinctured, drenched in empyrean light;
And in the meadows and the lower grounds
Was all the sweetness of a common dawn –
Dews, vapours, and the melody of birds,
And labourers going forth into the fields.
Ah, need I say, dear friend, that to the brim
My heart was full? I made no vows, but vows
Were then made for me: bond unknown to me
Was given, that I should be – else sinning greatly –
A dedicated spirit. On I walked
In blessedness, which even yet remains.

                    (*1805* iv, 319–45)

Crossing the Alps
1790

                              Upturning with a band
Of travellers, from the Valais we had climbed
Along the road that leads to Italy;
A length of hours, making of these our guides,
Did we advance, and, having reached an inn
Among the mountains, we together ate
Our noon's repast, from which the travellers rose
Leaving us at the board. Erelong we followed,
Descending by the beaten road that led
Right to a rivulet's edge, and there broke off;
The only track now visible was one
Upon the further side, right opposite,
And up a lofty mountain. This we took,
After a little scruple and short pause,
And climbed with eagerness – though not, at length,
Without surprise and some anxiety
On finding that we did not overtake
Our comrades gone before.
                              By fortunate chance,
While every moment now increased our doubts,
A peasant met us, and from him we learned
That to the place which had perplexed us first
We must descend, and there should find the road
Which in the stony channel of the stream
Lay a few steps, and then along its banks –
And further, that thenceforward all our course
Was downwards with the current of that stream.
Hard of belief, we questioned him again,
And all the answers which the man returned
To our enquiries, in their sense and substance
Translated by the feelings which we had,
Ended in this – that we had crossed the Alps.
    Imagination! – lifting up itself

dumb cataracts and streams of ice –
A motionless array of mighty waves,
Five rivers broad and vast . . .

The Source of the Aveyron, Francis Towne, 1781 (Denys Oppé).

Before the eye and progress of my song
Like an unfathered vapour, here that power,
In all the might of its endowments, came
Athwart me. I was lost as in a cloud,
Halted without a struggle to break through;
And now, recovering, to my soul I say
'I recognise thy glory'.
                              In such strength
Of usurpation, in such visitings
Of awful promise, when the light of sense
Goes out in flashes that have shown to us
The invisible world, doth greatness make abode,
There harbours whether we be young or old.
Our destiny, our nature, and our home,
Is with infinitude – and only there;
With hope it is, hope that can never die,
Effort, and expectation, and desire,
And something evermore about to be.
The mind beneath such banners militant
Thinks not of spoils or trophies, nor of aught
That may attest its prowess, blessed in thoughts
That are their own perfection and reward –
Strong in itself, and in the access of joy
Which hides it like the overflowing Nile.
    The dull and heavy slackening which ensued
Upon those tidings by the peasant given
Was soon dislodged; downwards we hurried fast,
And entered with the road which we had missed
Into a narrow chasm. The brook and road
Were fellow-travellers in this gloomy pass,
And with them did we journey several hours
At a slow step.
                    The immeasurable height
Of woods decaying, never to be decayed,
The stationary blasts of waterfalls,
And everywhere along the hollow rent
Winds thwarting winds, bewildered and forlorn,

The torrents shooting from the clear blue sky,
The rocks that muttered close upon our ears –
Black drizzling crags that spake by the wayside
As if a voice were in them – the sick sight
And giddy prospect of the raving stream,
The unfettered clouds and region of the heavens,
Tumult and peace, the darkness and the light,
Were all like workings of one mind, the features
Of the same face, blossoms upon one tree,
Characters of the great apocalypse,
The types and symbols of eternity,
Of first, and last, and midst, and without end.

(*1805* vi, 494–572)

The Climbing of Snowdon

It was a summer's night, a close warm night,
Wan, dull, and glaring, with a dripping mist
Low-hung and thick that covered all the sky,
Half threatening storm and rain; but on we went
Unchecked, being full of heart and having faith
In our tried pilot. Little could we see,
Hemmed round on every side with fog and damp,
And, after ordinary travellers' chat
With our conductor, silently we sunk
Each into commerce with his private thoughts.
Thus did we breast the ascent, and by myself
Was nothing either seen or heard the while
Which took me from my musings, save that once
The shepherd's cur did to his own great joy
Unearth a hedgehog in the mountain-crags,
Round which he made a barking turbulent.
   This small adventure – for even such it seemed
In that wild place and at the dead of night –
Being over and forgotten, on we wound
In silence as before. With forehead bent
Earthward, as if in opposition set
Against an enemy, I panted up
With eager pace, and no less eager thoughts.
Thus might we wear perhaps an hour away,
Ascending at loose distance each from each,
And I, as chanced, the foremost of the band –
When at my feet the ground appeared to brighten,
And with a step or two seemed brighter still;
Nor had I time to ask the cause of this,
For instantly a light upon the turf
Fell like a flash.
                    I looked about, and lo,
The moon stood naked in the heavens at height
Immense above my head, and on the shore

49

I found myself of a huge sea of mist,
Which meek and silent rested at my feet.
A hundred hills their dusky backs upheaved
All over this still ocean, and beyond,
Far, far beyond, the vapours shot themselves
In headlands, tongues, and promontory shapes,
Into the sea – the real sea – that seemed
To dwindle and give up its majesty,
Usurped upon as far as sight could reach.
　　Meanwhile, the moon looked down upon this show
In single glory, and we stood, the mist
Touching our very feet; and from the shore
At distance not the third part of a mile
Was a blue chasm, a fracture in the vapour,
A deep and gloomy breathing-place, through which
Mounted the roar of waters, torrents, streams
Innumerable, roaring with one voice.
The universal spectacle throughout
Was shaped for admiration and delight,
Grand in itself alone, but in that breach
Through which the homeless voice of waters rose,
That dark deep thoroughfare, had Nature lodged
The soul, the imagination, of the whole.
　　A meditation rose in me that night
Upon the lonely mountain when the scene
Had passed away, and it appeared to me
The perfect image of a mighty mind,
Of one that feeds upon infinity,
That is exalted by an under-presence,
The sense of God, or whatsoe'er is dim
Or vast in its own being . . .

(*1805* xiii, 10–73)

Scenes from
the French Revolution

i. *Golden Hours*
Calais, July 1790

Bliss was it in that dawn to be alive,
But to be young was very heaven!

*   *   *

'Twas a time when Europe was rejoiced,
France standing on the top of golden hours,
And human nature seeming born again.
Bound, as I said, to the Alps, it was our lot
To land at Calais on the very eve
Of that great federal day; and there we saw,
In a mean city and among a few,
How bright a face is worn when joy of one
Is joy of tens of millions.
               Southward thence
We took our way, direct through hamlets, towns,
Gaudy with relics of that festival,
Flowers left to wither on triumphal arcs
And window-garlands. On the public roads
(And once three days successively through paths
By which our toilsome journey was abridged)
Among sequestered villages we walked,
And found benevolence and blessedness
Spread like a fragrance everywhere . . .

(1805 x, 692–3; vi, 352–69)

ii. *A Tourist's Unconcern*
Paris, December 1791

Where silent zephyrs sported with the dust
Of the Bastille I sat in the open sun
And from the rubbish gathered up a stone,
And pocketed the relic in the guise
Of an enthusiast; yet, in honest truth,
Though not without some strong incumbencies,
And glad – could living man be otherwise? –
I looked for something which I could not find,
Affecting more emotion than I felt . . .

(*1805* ix, 63–71)

iii. *Among Royalists*
Blois, Spring 1792

A knot of military officers
That to a regiment appertained which then
Was stationed in the city were the chief
Of my associates; some of these wore swords
Which had been seasoned in the wars, and all
Were men well-born – at least laid claim to such
Distinction, as the chivalry of France.
In age and temper differing, they had yet
One spirit ruling in them all – alike
(Save only one, hereafter to be named)
Were bent upon undoing what was done.
This was their rest, and only hope; therewith
No fear had they of bad becoming worse,
For worst to them was come – nor would have stirred,
Or deemed it worth a moment's while to stir,
In any thing, save only as the act
Looked thitherward.
      One, reckoning by years,
Was in the prime of manhood, and erewhile
He had sat lord in many tender hearts,
Though heedless of such honours now, and changed:
His temper was quite mastered by the times,
And they had blighted him, had eat away
The beauty of his person, doing wrong
Alike to body and to mind. His port,
Which once had been erect and open, now
Was stooping and contracted, and a face
By nature lovely in itself, expressed,
As much as any that was ever seen,
A ravage out of season, made by thoughts
Unhealthy and vexatious. At the hour,
The most important of each day, in which
The public news was read, the fever came,

A punctual visitant, to shake this man,
Disarmed his voice and fanned his yellow cheek
Into a thousand colours. While he read,
Or mused, his sword was haunted by his touch
Continually, like an uneasy place
In his own body.
                    'Twas in truth an hour
Of universal ferment – mildest men
Were agitated, and commotions, strife
Of passion and opinion, filled the walls
Of peaceful houses with unquiet sounds . . .

(*1805* ix, 127–68)

iv. *A Patriot*

Blois, Early Summer 1792

Among that band of officers was one,
Already hinted at, of other mould –
A patriot, thence rejected by the rest . . .
                   And when we chanced
One day to meet a hunger-bitten girl
Who crept along fitting her languid self
Unto a heifer's motion – by a cord
Tied to her arm, and picking thus from the lane
Its sustenance, while the girl with her two hands
Was busy knitting in a heartless mood
Of solitude – and at the sight my friend
In agitation said, ' 'Tis against that
Which we are fighting', I with him believed
Devoutly that a spirit was abroad
Which could not be withstood, that poverty,
At least like this, would in a little time
Be found no more, that we should see the earth
Unthwarted in her wish to recompense
The industrious, and the lowly child of toil,
All institutes for ever blotted out
That legalised exclusion, empty pomp
Abolished, sensual state and cruel power,
Whether by edict of the one or few –
And finally, as sum and crown of all,
Should see the people having a strong hand
In making their own laws, whence better days
To all mankind.

                (*1805* ix, 294–6, 511–34)

v. *Sleep no More*
Paris, October 1792

My room was high and lonely, near the roof
Of a large mansion or hotel, a spot
That would have pleased me in more quiet times –
Nor was it wholly without pleasure then.
With unextinguished taper I kept watch,
Reading at intervals. The fear gone by
Pressed on me almost like a fear to come.
I thought of those September massacres,
Divided from me by a little month,
And felt and touched them, a substantial dread . . .
   'The horse is taught his manage, and the wind
Of heaven wheels round and treads in his own steps;
Year follows year, the tide returns again,
Day follows day, all things have second birth;
The earthquake is not satisfied at once' –
And in such way I wrought upon myself,
Until I seemed to hear a voice that cried
To the whole city, 'Sleep no more!' To this
Add comments of a calmer mind (from which
I could not gather full security),
But at the best it seemed a place of fear,
Unfit for the repose of night,
Defenceless as a wood where tigers roam.

(1805 x, 57–82)

vi. *War and Alienation*
London, 1793–4

'Twas not concealed with what ungracious eyes
Our native rulers from the very first
Had looked upon regenerated France . . .
                   I, who with the breeze
Had played, a green leaf on the blessed tree
Of my beloved country (nor had wished
For happier fortune than to wither there),
Now from my pleasant station was cut off,
And tossed about in whirlwinds. I rejoiced –
Yea, afterwards, truth painful to record,
Exulted in the triumph of my soul –
When Englishmen by thousands were o'erthrown,
Left without glory on the field, or driven,
Brave hearts, to shameful flight.
                       It was a grief –
Grief call it not, 'twas any thing but that –
A conflict of sensations without name,
Of which he only who may love the sight
Of a village-steeple as I do can judge,
When in the congregation, bending all
To their great Father, prayers were offered up
Or praises for our country's victories,
And, mid the simple worshippers perchance
I only, like an uninvited guest
Whom no one owned, sat silent – shall I add,
Fed on the day of vengeance yet to come!

               (*1805* x, 242–4, 253–74)

vii. *Eternal Justice*
Morecambe Sands, August 1794

O friend, few happier moments have been mine
Through my whole life than that when first I heard
That this foul tribe of Moloch was o'erthrown,
And their chief regent levelled with the dust . . .
  Without me and within as I advanced
All that I saw, or felt, or communed with,
Was gentleness and peace. Upon a small
And rocky island near, a fragment stood –
Itself like a sea rock – of what had been
A Romish chapel, where in ancient times
Masses were said at the hour which suited those
Who crossed the sands with ebb of morning tide.
Not far from this still ruin all the plain
Was spotted with a variegated crowd
Of coaches, wains, and travellers, horse and foot,
Wading, beneath the conduct of their guide,
In loose procession through the shallow stream
Of inland water; the great sea meanwhile
Was at safe distance, far retired.
                                        I paused,
Unwilling to proceed, the scene appeared
So gay and cheerful – when, a traveller
Chancing to pass, I carelessly enquired
If any news were stirring; he replied
In the familiar language of the day
That *Robespierre was dead*. Nor was a doubt,
On further question, left within my mind
But that the tidings were substantial truth –
That he and his supporters all were fallen.
  Great was my glee of spirit, great my joy
In vengeance, and eternal justice, thus
Made manifest. 'Come now, ye golden times',
Said I, forth-breathing on those open sands

A hymn of triumph, 'as the morning comes
Out of the bosom of the night, come ye!
Thus far our trust is verified: behold,
They who with clumsy desperation brought
Rivers of blood, and preached that nothing else
Could cleanse the Augean stable, by the might
Of their own helper have been swept away . . .'

(*1805* x, 466–9, 515–49)

viii. *Confusion and Recovery*
Racedown, Spring 1796

                Time may come
When some dramatic story may afford
Shapes livelier to convey to thee, my friend,
What then I learned – or think I learned – of truth,
And the errors into which I was betrayed
By present objects, and by reasonings false
From the beginning, inasmuch as drawn
Out of a heart which had been turned aside
From Nature by external accidents,
And which was thus confounded more and more,
Misguiding and misguided.
                Thus I fared,
Dragging all passions, notions, shapes of faith,
Like culprits to the bar, suspiciously
Calling the mind to establish in plain day
Her titles and her honours, now believing,
Now disbelieving, endlessly perplexed
With impulse, motive, right and wrong, the ground
Of moral obligation – what the rule,
And what the sanction – till, demanding proof,
And seeking it in every thing, I lost
All feeling of conviction, and, in fine,
Sick, wearied out with contrarieties,
Yielded up moral questions in despair,
And for my future studies, as the sole
Employment of the enquiring faculty,
Turned towards mathematics, and their clear
And solid evidence.
                Ah, then it was
That thou, most precious friend, about this time
First known to me, didst lend a living help
To regulate my soul. And then it was
That the beloved woman in whose sight

The forces of reaction. A 'Church and King' mob in Birmingham at work on the house of a leading dissenter, Joseph Priestley, 14 July 1791. Johann Eckstein (Susan Lowndes Marques).

Those days were past – now speaking in a voice
Of sudden admonition like a brook
That does but cross a lonely road; and now
Seen, heard and felt, and caught at every turn,
Companion never lost through many a league –
Maintained for me a saving intercourse
With my true self (for, though impaired and changed –
Much, as it seemed – I was no further changed
Than as a clouded, not a waning moon);
She, in the midst of all, preserved me still
A poet, made me seek beneath that name
My office upon earth, and nowhere else.

(*1805* x, 878–920)

Bartholomew Fair

For once the Muse's help will we implore,
And she shall lodge us (wafted on her wings
Above the press and danger of the crowd)
Upon some showman's platform. What a hell
For eyes and ears! What anarchy and din
Barbarian and infernal! – 'tis a dream
Monstrous in colour, motion, shape, sight, sound.
    Below, the open space, through every nook
Of the wide area, twinkles, is alive
With heads; the midway region and above
Is thronged with staring pictures and huge scrolls,
Dumb proclamations of the prodigies:
And chattering monkeys dangling from their poles,
And children whirling in their roundabouts;
With those that stretch the neck, and strain the eyes,
And crack the voice in rivalship, the crowd
Inviting; with buffoons against buffoons
Grimacing, writhing, screaming; him who grinds
The hurdy-gurdy, at the fiddle weaves,
Rattles the salt-box, thumps the kettle-drum,
And him who at the trumpet puffs his cheeks,
The silver-collared negro with his timbrel,
Equestrians, tumblers, women, girls, and boys,
Blue-breeched, pink-vested, and with towering plumes.
    All moveables of wonder from all parts
Are here, albinos, painted Indians, dwarfs,
The horse of knowledge, and the learned pig,
The stone-eater, the man that swallows fire,
Giants, ventriloquists, the invisible girl,
The bust that speaks and moves its goggling eyes,
The waxwork, clockwork, all the marvellous craft
Of modern Merlins, wild beasts, puppet-shows,
All out-of-the-way, far-fetched, perverted things,
All freaks of Nature, all Promethean thoughts

Of man – his dullness, madness, and their feats,
All jumbled up together to make up
This parliament of monsters. Tents and booths
Meanwhile – as if the whole were one vast mill –
Are vomiting, receiving, on all sides,
Men, women, three-years' children, babes in arms.

(*1805* vii, *656–95*)

The London Beggar

How often in the overflowing streets
Have I gone forwards with the crowd, and said
Unto myself, 'The face of every one
That passes by me is a mystery.'
Thus have I looked, nor ceased to look (oppressed
By thoughts of what, and whither, when and how),
Until the shapes before my eyes became
A second-sight procession, such as glides
Over still mountains, or appears in dreams,
And all the ballast of familiar life –
The present, and the past, hope, fear, all stays,
All laws of acting, thinking, speaking man –
Went from me, neither knowing me, nor known.
    And once, far travelled in such mood, beyond
The reach of common indications, lost
Amid the moving pageant, 'twas my chance
Abruptly to be smitten with the view
Of a blind beggar, who, with upright face,
Stood propped against a wall, upon his chest
Wearing a written paper, to explain
The story of the man, and who he was.
My mind did at this spectacle turn round
As with the might of waters, and it seemed
To me that in this label was a type
Or emblem of the utmost that we know
Both of ourselves and of the universe,
And on the shape of this unmoving man,
His fixed face and sightless eyes, I looked,
As if admonished from another world.

(*1805* vii, *595–623*)

a blind beggar, who, with upright face,
Stood propped against a wall, upon his chest
Wearing a written paper, to explain
The story of the man, and who he was . . .

Giving Alms, Thomas Rowlandson, 1758–1827 (Wordsworth
Trust).

Old Man Travelling

                        The little hedge-row birds
That peck along the road, regard him not;
He travels on, and in his face, his step,
His gait, is one expression. Every limb,
His look and bending figure, all bespeak
A man who does not move with pain, but moves
With thought. He is insensibly subdued
To settled quiet, he is one by whom
All effort seems forgotten – one to whom
Long patience has such mild composure given,
That patience now doth seem a thing of which
He hath no need. He is by Nature led
To peace so perfect that the young behold
With envy what the old man hardly feels.

The Ruined Cottage

'Twas summer, and the sun was mounted high;
Along the south the uplands feebly glared
Through a pale steam, and all the northern downs –
In clearer air ascending – showed far off
Their surfaces with shadows dappled o'er
Of deep embattled clouds. Far as the sight
Could reach those many shadows lay in spots
Determined and unmoved, with steady beams
Of clear and pleasant sunshine interposed –
Pleasant to him who on the soft cool moss
Extends his careless limbs beside the root
Of some huge oak whose aged branches make
A twilight of their own, a dewy shade
Where the wren warbles while the dreaming man
(Half-conscious of that soothing melody)
With side-long eye looks out upon the scene,
By those impending branches made more soft,
More soft and distant.
               Other lot was mine.
Across a bare wide common I had toiled
With languid feet which by the slippery ground
Were baffled still; and when I stretched myself
On the brown earth my limbs from very heat
Could find no rest, nor my weak arm disperse
The insect host which gathered round my face
And joined their murmurs to the tedious noise
Of seeds of bursting gorse that crackled round.
I rose and turned towards a group of trees
Which midway in that level stood alone;
And thither come at length, beneath a shade
Of clustering elms that sprang from the same root
I found a ruined house, four naked walls
That stared upon each other. I looked round,

And near the door I saw an aged man
Alone and stretched upon the cottage-bench;
An iron-pointed staff lay at his side.
With instantaneous joy I recognised
That pride of Nature and of lowly life,
The venerable Armytage, a friend
As dear to me as is the setting sun.
                                Two days before
We had been fellow-travellers: I knew
That he was in this neighbourhood, and now
Delighted found him here in the cool shade.
He lay, his pack of rustic merchandise
Pillowing his head. I guess he had no thought
Of his way-wandering life. His eyes were shut,
The shadows of the breezy elms above
Dappled his face. With thirsty heat oppressed
At length I hailed him, glad to see his hat
Bedewed with water-drops, as if the brim
Had newly scooped a running stream. He rose
And pointing to a sun-flower, bade me climb
The broken wall where that same gaudy flower
Looked out upon the road.
                                It was a plot
Of garden-ground now wild, its matted weeds
Marked with the steps of those whom (as they passed)
The gooseberry-trees that shot in long lank slips,
Or currants hanging from their leafless stems
In scanty strings, had tempted to o'erleap
The broken wall. Within that cheerless spot,
Where two tall hedgerows of thick alder boughs
Joined in a damp cold nook, I found a well
Half covered up with willow-flowers and grass.
I slaked my thirst and to the shady bench
Returned, and while I stood unbonneted
To catch the motion of the cooler air
The old man said, 'I see around me here
Things which you cannot see. We die, my friend,

Nor we alone, but that which each man loved
And prized in his peculiar nook of earth
Dies with him, or is changed, and very soon
Even of the good is no memorial left.

   The poets, in their elegies and songs
Lamenting the departed, call the groves,
They call upon the hills and streams to mourn,
And senseless rocks – nor idly, for they speak
In these their invocations with a voice
Obedient to the strong creative power
Of human passion. Sympathies there are
More tranquil, yet perhaps of kindred birth,
That steal upon the meditative mind
And grow with thought. Beside yon spring I stood,
And eyed its waters till we seemed to feel
One sadness, they and I. For them a bond
Of brotherhood is broken: time has been
When every day the touch of human hand
Disturbed their stillness, and they ministered
To human comfort. When I stooped to drink
A spider's web hung to the water's edge,
And on the wet and slimy foot-stone lay
The useless fragment of a wooden bowl.
It moved my very heart.

                 The day has been
When I could never pass this road but she
Who lived within these walls, when I appeared,
A daughter's welcome gave me, and I loved her
As my own child. Oh sir, the good die first,
And they whose hearts are dry as summer dust
Burn to the socket! Many a passenger
Has blessed poor Margaret for her gentle looks
When she upheld the cool refreshment drawn
From that forsaken spring, and no one came
But he was welcome, no one went away
But that it seemed she loved him.

                   She is dead,

The worm is on her cheek, and this poor hut,
Stripped of its outward garb of household flowers –
Of rose and sweetbriar – offers to the wind
A cold bare wall whose earthy top is tricked
With weeds and the rank speargrass. She is dead,
And nettles rot and adders sun themselves
Where we have sat together while she nursed
Her infant at her breast. The unshod colt,
The wandering heifer and the potter's ass,
Find shelter now within the chimney-wall
Where I have seen her evening hearthstone blaze
And through the window spread upon the road
Its cheerful light. You will forgive me, sir,
But often on this cottage do I muse
As on a picture, till my wiser mind
Sinks, yielding to the foolishness of grief.
    She had a husband, an industrious man,
Sober and steady. I have heard her say
That he was up and busy at his loom
In summer ere the mower's scythe had swept
The dewy grass, and in the early spring
Ere the last star had vanished. They who passed
At evening, from behind the garden-fence
Might hear his busy spade, which he would ply
After his daily work till the daylight
Was gone, and every leaf and flower were lost
In the dark hedges. So they passed their days
In peace and comfort, and two pretty babes
Were their best hope next to the God in heaven.
    You may remember, now some ten years gone,
Two blighting seasons when the fields were left
With half a harvest. It pleased heaven to add
A worse affliction in the plague of war;
A happy land was stricken to the heart –
'Twas a sad time of sorrow and distress!
A wanderer among the cottages,
I (with my pack of winter raiment) saw

The hardships of that season. Many rich
Sunk down as in a dream among the poor,
And of the poor did many cease to be,
And their place knew them not.
                              Meanwhile – abridged
Of daily comforts, gladly reconciled
To numerous self-denials – Margaret
Went struggling on through those calamitous years
With cheerful hope. But ere the second autumn,
A fever seized her husband. In disease
He lingered long, and when his strength returned
He found the little he had stored to meet
The hour of accident, or crippling age,
Was all consumed. As I have said, 'twas now
A time of trouble: shoals of artisans
Were from their daily labour turned away
To hang for bread on parish charity,
They and their wives and children – happier far
Could they have lived as do the little birds
That peck along the hedges, or the kite
That makes her dwelling in the mountain-rocks.
    Ill fared it now with Robert, he who dwelt
In this poor cottage. At his door he stood
And whistled many a snatch of merry tunes
That had no mirth in them, or with his knife
Carved uncouth figures on the heads of sticks;
Then idly sought about through every nook
Of house or garden any casual task
Of use or ornament, and with a strange
Amusing but uneasy novelty
He blended where he might the various tasks
Of summer, autumn, winter, and of spring.
But this endured not, his good humour soon
Became a weight in which no pleasure was,
And poverty brought on a petted mood
And a sore temper. Day by day he drooped,
And he would leave his home, and to the town

beneath a shade
Of clustering elms that sprang from the same root
I found a ruined house, four naked walls
That stared upon each other.

Birket Foster, engraved frontispiece to the first separate publication of Wordsworth's poem (as *The Deserted Cottage*), 1859.

75

Without an errand would he turn his steps,
Or wander here and there among the fields.
One while he would speak lightly of his babes
And with a cruel tongue, at other times
He played with them wild freaks of merriment,
And 'twas a piteous thing to see the looks
Of the poor innocent children. "Every smile",
Said Margaret to me here beneath these trees,
"Made my heart bleed." '

                       At this the old man paused,
And looking up to those enormous elms
He said, ' 'Tis now the hour of deepest noon.
At this still season of repose and peace,
This hour when all things which are not at rest
Are cheerful, while this multitude of flies
Fills all the air with happy melody,
Why should a tear be in an old man's eye?
Why should we thus with an untoward mind,
And in the weakness of humanity,
From natural wisdom turn our hearts away,
To natural comfort shut our eyes and ears,
And, feeding on disquiet, thus disturb
The calm of Nature with our restless thoughts?'

Second Part

He spake with somewhat of a solemn tone,
But when he ended there was in his face
Such easy cheerfulness, a look so mild,
That for a little time it stole away
All recollection, and that simple tale
Passed from my mind like a forgotten sound.
A while on trivial things we held discourse,
To me soon tasteless: in my own despite
I thought of that poor woman as of one
Whom I had known and loved. He had rehearsed
Her homely tale with such familiar power,
With such an active countenance, an eye

So busy, that the things of which he spake
Seemed present, and (attention now relaxed)
There was a heartfelt chillness in my veins.
I rose, and turning from that breezy shade
Went out into the open air, and stood
To drink the comfort of the warmer sun.
Long time I had not stayed ere, looking round
Upon that tranquil ruin, I returned
And begged of the old man that for my sake
He would resume his story.
                              He replied,
'It were a wantonness, and would demand
Severe reproof, if we were men whose hearts
Could hold vain dalliance with the misery
Even of the dead, contented thence to draw
A momentary pleasure, never marked
By reason, barren of all future good.
But we have known that there is often found
In mournful thoughts – and always might be found –
A power to virtue friendly. Were't not so
I am a dreamer among men, indeed
An idle dreamer. 'Tis a common tale
By moving accidents uncharactered,
A tale of silent suffering, hardly clothed
In bodily form, and to the grosser sense
But ill adapted – scarcely palpable
To him who does not think. But at your bidding
I will proceed.
                   While thus it fared with them
To whom this cottage till that hapless year
Had been a blessed home, it was my chance
To travel in a country far remote;
And glad I was when, halting by yon gate
That leads from the green lane, again I saw
These lofty elm-trees. Long I did not rest –
With many pleasant thoughts I cheered my way
O'er the flat common. At the door arrived,

I knocked, and when I entered, with the hope
Of usual greeting, Margaret looked at me
A little while, then turned her head away
Speechless, and sitting down upon a chair
Wept bitterly. I wist not what to do,
Or how to speak to her. Poor wretch, at last
She rose from off her seat, and then, oh sir,
I cannot tell how she pronounced my name!
With fervent love, and with a face of grief
Unutterably helpless, and a look
That seemed to cling upon me, she enquired
If I had seen her husband.
                                         As she spake
A strange surprise and fear came to my heart,
Nor had I power to answer ere she told
That he had disappeared – just two months gone.
He left his house: two wretched days had passed,
And on the third by the first break of light,
Within her casement full in view she saw
A purse of gold. "I trembled at the sight",
Said Margaret, "for I knew it was his hand
That placed it there. And on that very day
By one, a stranger, from my husband sent,
The tidings came that he had joined a troop
Of soldiers going to a distant land.
He left me thus. Poor man, he had not heart
To take a farewell of me, and he feared
That I should follow with my babes, and sink
Beneath the misery of a soldier's life."
    This tale did Margaret tell with many tears,
And when she ended I had little power
To give her comfort, and was glad to take
Such words of hope from her own mouth as served
To cheer us both. But long we had not talked
Ere we built up a pile of better thoughts,
And with a brighter eye she looked around
As if she had been shedding tears of joy.

We parted. It was then the early spring;
I left her busy with her garden tools,
And well remember, o'er that fence she looked,
And, while I paced along the foot-way path,
Called out and sent a blessing after me
With tender cheerfulness, and with a voice
That seemed the very sound of happy thoughts.
   I roved o'er many a hill and many a dale
With this my weary load, in heat and cold,
Through many a wood and many an open ground,
In sunshine or in shade, in wet or fair,
Now blithe, now drooping, as it might befall;
My best companions now the driving winds
And now the "trotting brooks" and whispering trees,
And now the music of my own sad steps,
With many a short-lived thought that passed between
And disappeared.
            I came this way again
Towards the wane of summer, when the wheat
Was yellow, and the soft and bladed grass
Sprang up afresh and o'er the hayfield spread
Its tender green. When I had reached the door
I found that she was absent. In the shade,
Where we now sit, I waited her return.
Her cottage in its outward look appeared
As cheerful as before, in any show
Of neatness little changed – but that I thought
The honeysuckle crowded round the door
And from the wall hung down in heavier tufts,
And knots of worthless stonecrop started out
Along the window's edge, and grew like weeds
Against the lower panes. I turned aside
And strolled into her garden. It was changed.
The unprofitable bindweed spread his bells
From side to side, and with unwieldy wreaths
Had dragged the rose from its sustaining wall
And bent it down to earth. The border tufts –

Daisy, and thrift, and lowly camomile,
And thyme – had straggled out into the paths
Which they were used to deck.

                    Ere this an hour
Was wasted. Back I turned my restless steps,
And as I walked before the door it chanced
A stranger passed, and, guessing whom I sought,
He said that she was used to ramble far.
The sun was sinking in the west, and now
I sat with sad impatience. From within
Her solitary infant cried aloud.
The spot though fair seemed very desolate –
The longer I remained more desolate –
And looking round I saw the corner-stones,
Till then unmarked, on either side the door
With dull red stains discoloured, and stuck o'er
With tufts and hairs of wool, as if the sheep
That feed upon the commons thither came
Familiarly, and found a couching-place
Even at her threshold.

               The house-clock struck eight:
I turned and saw her distant a few steps.
Her face was pale and thin, her figure too
Was changed. As she unlocked the door she said,
"It grieves me you have waited here so long,
But in good truth I've wandered much of late,
And sometimes – to my shame I speak – have need
Of my best prayers to bring me back again."
While on the board she spread our evening meal
She told me she had lost her elder child,
That he for months had been a serving-boy,
Apprenticed by the parish. "I perceive
You look at me, and you have cause. Today
I have been travelling far, and many days
About the fields I wander, knowing this
Only, that what I seek I cannot find.
And so I waste my time: for I am changed,

And to myself", said she, "have done much wrong,
And to this helpless infant. I have slept
Weeping, and weeping I have waked. My tears
Have flowed as if my body were not such
As others are, and I could never die.
But I am now in mind and in my heart
More easy, and I hope", said she, "that heaven
Will give me patience to endure the things
Which I behold at home."
                              It would have grieved
Your very soul to see her. Sir, I feel
The story linger in my heart; I fear
'Tis long and tedious, but my spirit clings
To that poor woman. So familiarly
Do I perceive her manner and her look
And presence, and so deeply do I feel
Her goodness, that not seldom in my walks
A momentary trance comes over me
And to myself I seem to muse on one
By sorrow laid asleep or borne away,
A human being destined to awake
To human life – or something very near
To human life – when he shall come again
For whom she suffered.
                              Sir, it would have grieved
Your very soul to see her: evermore
Her eyelids drooped, her eyes were downward cast;
And when she at her table gave me food
She did not look at me. Her voice was low,
Her body was subdued. In every act
Pertaining to her house-affairs appeared
The careless stillness which a thinking mind
Gives to an idle matter. Still she sighed,
But yet no motion of the breast was seen,
No heaving of the heart. While by the fire
We sat together, sighs came on my ear –
I knew not how, and hardly whence, they came.

My best companions now the driving winds,
And now the 'trotting brooks' and whispering trees,
And now the music of my own sad steps . . .

The Shore of Keswick Lake, Ramsay Richard Reinagle, 1775–1862
(Laing Art Gallery).

I took my staff, and when I kissed her babe
The tears stood in her eyes. I left her then
With the best hope and comfort I could give:
She thanked me for my will, but for my hope
It seemed she did not thank me.
                                        I returned
And took my rounds along this road again
Ere on its sunny bank the primrose flower
Had chronicled the earliest day of spring.
I found her sad and drooping. She had learned
No tidings of her husband. If he lived,
She knew not that he lived: if he were dead,
She knew not he was dead. She seemed the same
In person or appearance, but her house
Bespoke a sleepy hand of negligence.
The floor was neither dry nor neat, the hearth
Was comfortless,
The windows too were dim, and her few books,
Which one upon the other heretofore
Had been piled up against the corner-panes
In seemly order, now with straggling leaves
Lay scattered here and there, open or shut,
As they had chanced to fall. Her infant babe
Had from its mother caught the trick of grief,
And sighed amongst its playthings.
                                        Once again
I turned towards the garden-gate, and saw
More plainly still that poverty and grief
Were now come nearer to her. The earth was hard,
With weeds defaced and knots of withered grass;
No ridges there appeared of clear black mould,
No winter greenness. Of her herbs and flowers
It seemed the better part were gnawed away
Or trampled on the earth. A chain of straw,
Which had been twisted round the tender stem
Of a young appletree, lay at its root;
The bark was nibbled round by truant sheep.

Margaret stood near, her infant in her arms,
And, seeing that my eye was on the tree,
She said, "I fear it will be dead and gone
Ere Robert come again."
                              Towards the house
Together we returned, and she enquired
If I had any hope. But for her babe,
And for her little friendless boy, she said,
She had no wish to live – that she must die
Of sorrow. Yet I saw the idle loom
Still in its place. His Sunday garments hung
Upon the self-same nail, his very staff
Stood undisturbed behind the door. And when
I passed this way beaten by autumn winds,
She told me that her little babe was dead
And she was left alone. That very time,
I yet remember, through the miry lane
She walked with me a mile, when the bare trees
Trickled with foggy damps, and in such sort
That any heart had ached to hear her, begged
That wheresoe'er I went I still would ask
For him whom she had lost. We parted then,
Our final parting; for from that time forth
Did many seasons pass ere I returned
Into this tract again.
                              Five tedious years
She lingered in unquiet widowhood,
A wife and widow. Needs must it have been
A sore heart-wasting. I have heard, my friend,
That in that broken arbour she would sit
The idle length of half a sabbath day –
There, where you see the toadstool's lazy head –
And when a dog passed by she still would quit
The shade and look abroad. On this old bench
For hours she sat, and evermore her eye
Was busy in the distance, shaping things
Which made her heart beat quick. Seest thou that path

(The green-sward now has broken its grey line)?
There to and fro she paced through many a day
Of the warm summer, from a belt of flax
That girt her waist, spinning the long-drawn thread
With backward steps. Yet ever as there passed
A man whose garments shewed the soldier's red,
Or crippled mendicant in sailor's garb,
The little child who sat to turn the wheel
Ceased from his toil, and she, with faltering voice,
Expecting still to learn her husband's fate,
Made many a fond enquiry; and when they
Whose presence gave no comfort, were gone by,
Her heart was still more sad. And by yon gate,
Which bars the traveller's road, she often stood,
And when a stranger horseman came, the latch
Would lift, and in his face look wistfully,
Most happy if from aught discovered there
Of tender feeling she might dare repeat
The same sad question.
                              Meanwhile her poor hut
Sunk to decay; for he was gone, whose hand
At the first nippings of October frost
Closed up each chink, and with fresh bands of straw
Chequered the green-grown thatch. And so she lived
Through the long winter, reckless and alone,
Till this reft house, by frost, and thaw, and rain,
Was sapped; and when she slept, the nightly damps
Did chill her breast, and in the stormy day
Her tattered clothes were ruffled by the wind
Even at the side of her own fire. Yet still
She loved this wretched spot, nor would for worlds
Have parted hence; and still that length of road,
And this rude bench, one torturing hope endeared,
Fast rooted at her heart. And here, my friend,
In sickness she remained; and here she died,
Last human tenant of these ruined walls.'
    The old man ceased; he saw that I was moved.

From that low bench rising instinctively,
I turned aside in weakness, nor had power
To thank him for the tale which he had told.
I stood, and leaning o'er the garden-gate
Reviewed that woman's sufferings; and it seemed
To comfort me while with a brother's love
I blessed her in the impotence of grief.
At length towards the cottage I returned
Fondly, and traced with milder interest
That secret spirit of humanity
Which, mid the calm oblivious tendencies
Of Nature, mid her plants, her weeds and flowers,
And silent overgrowings, still survived.

The old man seeing this resumed, and said,
'My friend, enough to sorrow have you given,
The purposes of wisdom ask no more:
Be wise and cheerful, and no longer read
The forms of things with an unworthy eye.
She sleeps in the calm earth, and peace is here.
I well remember that those very plumes,
Those weeds, and the high speargrass on that wall,
By mist and silent raindrops silvered o'er,
As once I passed did to my mind convey
So still an image of tranquillity –
So calm and still, and looked so beautiful
Amid the uneasy thoughts which filled my mind –
That what we feel of sorrow and despair
From ruin and from change, and all the grief
The passing shows of being leave behind,
Appeared an idle dream that could not live
Where meditation was. I turned away,
And walked along my road in happiness.'

He ceased. By this the sun declining shot
A slant and mellow radiance, which began
To fall upon us where beneath the trees
We sat on that low bench. And now we felt,
Admonished thus, the sweet hour coming on:

A linnet warbled from those lofty elms,
A thrush sang loud, and other melodies
At distance heard peopled the milder air.
The old man rose and hoisted up his load;
Together casting then a farewell look
Upon those silent walls, we left the shade,
And ere the stars were visible attained
A rustic inn, our evening resting-place.

A Night-Piece

　　　　　　　　　The sky is overspread
With a close veil of one continuous cloud
All whitened by the moon, that just appears,
A dim-seen orb, yet chequers not the ground
With any shadow – plant, or tower, or tree.
At last a pleasant instantaneous light
Startles the musing man whose eyes are bent
To earth. He looks around, the clouds are split
Asunder, and above his head he views
The clear moon and the glory of the heavens.
　There in a black-blue vault she sails along
Followed by multitudes of stars, that small,
And bright, and sharp, along the gloomy vault
Drive as she drives. How fast they wheel away –
Yet vanish not! The wind is in the trees;
But they are silent. Still they roll along
Immeasurably distant, and the vault,
Built round by those white clouds, enormous clouds,
Still deepens its interminable depth.
At length the vision closes, and the mind
(Not undisturbed by the deep joy it feels,
Which slowly settles into peaceful calm)
Is left to muse upon the solemn scene.

In Storm and Tempest

In storm and tempest, and beneath the beam
Of quiet moons, he wandered there – and there
Would feel whate'er there is of power in sound
To breathe an elevated mood, by form
Or image unprofaned. There would he stand
Beneath some rock listening to sounds that are
The ghostly language of the ancient earth,
Or make their dim abode in distant winds;
Thence did he drink the visionary power.
I deem not profitless these fleeting moods
Of shadowy exaltation: not for this,
That they are kindred to our purer mind
And intellectual life, but that the soul –
Remembering how she felt, but what she felt
Remembering not – retains an obscure sense
Of possible sublimity, at which
With growing faculties she doth aspire,
With faculties still growing, feeling still
That whatsoever point they gain, there still
Is something to pursue.

                              But from these haunts
Of lonesome Nature he had skill to draw
A better and less transitory power,
An influence more habitual: to his mind
The mountain's outline and its steady form
Gave simple grandeur, and its presence shaped
The measure and the prospect of his soul
To majesty. Such virtue had the forms
Perennial of the ancient hills; nor less
The changeful language of their countenance
Gave movement to his thoughts, and multitude,
With order and relation.

'Put on with speed your woodland dress' – the only known likeness of Dorothy Wordsworth as a young woman (Wordsworth Trust).

To My Sister

It is the first mild day of March,
Each minute sweeter than before;
The redbreast sings from the tall larch
That stands beside our door.

There is a blessing in the air
Which seems a sense of joy to yield
To the bare trees, and mountains bare,
And grass in the green field.

My sister – 'tis a wish of mine –
Now that our morning meal is done,
Make haste, your morning task resign,
Come forth and feel the sun.

Edward will come with you, and pray
Put on with speed your woodland-dress,
And bring no book – for this one day
We'll give to idleness.

No joyless forms shall regulate
Our living calendar:
We from today, my friend, will date
The opening of the year.

Love, now an universal birth,
From heart to heart is stealing –
From earth to man, from man to earth –
It is the hour of feeling!

One moment now may give us more
Than fifty years of reason;
Our minds shall drink at every pore
The spirit of the season.

Some silent laws our hearts may make,
Which they shall long obey;
We for the year to come may take
Our temper from today.

And from the blessed power that rolls
About, below, above,
We'll frame the measure of our souls –
They shall be tuned to love.

Then come, my sister, come, I pray,
With speed put on your woodland-dress,
And bring no book, for this one day
We'll give to idleness.

Goody Blake and Harry Gill

Oh, what's the matter? What's the matter?
What is't that ails young Harry Gill,
That evermore his teeth they chatter,
Chatter, chatter, chatter still?
Of waistcoats Harry has no lack,
Good duffle grey, and flannel fine;
He has a blanket on his back,
And coats enough to smother nine.

In March, December, and in July,
'Tis all the same with Harry Gill –
The neighbours tell, and tell you truly,
His teeth they chatter, chatter still.
At night, at morning, and at noon,
'Tis all the same with Harry Gill;
Beneath the sun, beneath the moon,
His teeth they chatter, chatter still.

Young Harry was a lusty drover,
And who so stout of limb as he? –
His cheeks were red as ruddy clover,
His voice was like the voice of three.
Old Goody Blake was old and poor,
Ill fed she was, and thinly clad;
And any man who passed her door
Might see how poor a hut she had.

All day she spun in her poor dwelling,
And then her three hours' work at night!
Alas, 'twas hardly worth the telling –
It would not pay for candlelight.
This woman dwelt in Dorsetshire,
Her hut was on a cold hillside,
And in that country coals are dear,
For they come far by wind and tide.

By the same fire to boil their pottage,
Two poor dames (as I have known)
Will often live in one small cottage;
But she, poor woman, dwelt alone.
'Twas well enough when summer came –
The long, warm, lightsome summer day –
Then at her door the canty dame
Would sit, as any linnet gay.

But when the ice our streams did fetter,
Oh then how her old bones would shake!
You would have said, if you had met her,
'Twas a hard time for Goody Blake.
Her evenings then were dull and dead;
Sad case it was, as you may think,
For very cold to go to bed –
And then for cold not sleep a wink.

Oh joy for her, whene'er in winter
The winds at night had made a rout,
And scattered many a lusty splinter,
And many a rotten bough about.
Yet never had she, well or sick
(As every man who knew her says),
A pile beforehand, wood or stick,
Enough to warm her for three days.

Now, when the frost was past enduring
And made her poor old bones to ache,
Could any thing be more alluring
Than an old hedge to Goody Blake?
And now and then, it must be said,
When her old bones were cold and chill,
She left her fire, or left her bed,
To seek the hedge of Harry Gill.

Now Harry he had long suspected
This trespass of old Goody Blake,
And vowed that she should be detected,
And he on her would vengeance take.
And oft from his warm fire he'd go
And to the fields his road would take,
And there, at night, in frost and snow,
He watched to seize old Goody Blake.

And once, behind a rick of barley,
Thus looking out did Harry stand
(The moon was full and shining clearly,
And crisp with frost the stubble-land) –
He hears a noise, he's all awake!
Again? On tip-toe down the hill
He softly creeps – 'tis Goody Blake!
She's at the hedge of Harry Gill.

Right glad was he when he beheld her!
Stick after stick did Goody pull –
He stood behind a bush of elder,
Till she had filled her apron full.
When with her load she turned about,
The by-road back again to take,
He started forward with a shout,
And sprang upon poor Goody Blake.

And fiercely by the arm he took her,
And by the arm he held her fast,
And fiercely by the arm he shook her,
And cried, 'I've caught you then at last!'
Then Goody (who had nothing said)
Her bundle from her lap let fall,
And, kneeling on the sticks, she prayed
To God that is the judge of all.

She prayed, her withered hand uprearing,
While Harry held her by the arm:
'God, who art never out of hearing,
O may he never more be warm!'
The cold, cold moon above her head,
Thus on her knees did Goody pray;
Young Harry heard what she had said,
And icy-cold he turned away.

He went complaining all the morrow
That he was cold and very chill –
His face was gloom, his heart was sorrow –
Alas, that day for Harry Gill!
That day he wore a riding-coat,
But not a whit the warmer he;
Another was on Thursday brought,
And ere the sabbath he had three!

'Twas all in vain – a useless matter –
And blankets were about him pinned;
Yet still his jaws and teeth they clatter
Like a loose casement in the wind.
And Harry's flesh it fell away,
And all who see him say 'tis plain,
That, live as long as live he may,
He never will be warm again.

No word to any man he utters,
Abed or up, to young or old;
But ever to himself he mutters,
'Poor Harry Gill is very cold!'
Abed or up, by night or day,
His teeth they chatter, chatter still!
Now think, ye farmers all, I pray,
Of Goody Blake and Harry Gill.

The Thorn

'There is a thorn, it looks so old
In truth you'd find it hard to say
How it could ever have been young,
It looks so old and grey.
Not higher than a two years' child
It stands erect, this aged thorn;
No leaves it has, no thorny points —
It is a mass of knotted joints,
A wretched thing forlorn!
It stands erect, and like a stone
With lichens it is overgrown.

Like rock or stone, it is o'ergrown
With lichens to the very top,
And hung with heavy tufts of moss,
A melancholy crop.
Up from the earth these mosses creep,
And this poor thorn they clasp it round
So close you'd say that they were bent
With plain and manifest intent
To drag it to the ground,
And all had joined in one endeavour
To bury this poor thorn for ever!

High on a mountain's highest ridge
(Where oft the stormy winter gale
Cuts like a scythe, while through the clouds
It sweeps from vale to vale),
Not five yards from the mountain path
This thorn you on your left espy;
And to the left, three yards beyond,
You see a little muddy pond
Of water, never dry:
I've measured it from side to side,
'Tis three feet long and two feet wide.

And close beside this aged thorn
There is a fresh and lovely sight,
A beauteous heap, a hill of moss,
Just half a foot in height.
All lovely colours there you see,
All colours that were ever seen,
And mossy network too is there,
As if by hand of lady fair
The work had woven been –
And cups, the darlings of the eye,
So deep is their vermilion dye.

Ah me, what lovely tints are there
Of olive-green and scarlet bright,
In spikes, in branches, and in stars,
Green, red, and pearly white!
This heap of earth o'ergrown with moss,
Which close beside the thorn you see
So fresh in all its beauteous dyes,
Is like an infant's grave in size –
As like as like can be –
But never, never, anywhere
An infant's grave was half so fair.

Now would you see this aged thorn,
This pond and beauteous hill of moss,
You must take care and choose your time
The mountain when to cross.
For oft there sits, between the heap
That's like an infant's grave in size
And that same pond of which I spoke,
A woman in a scarlet cloak,
And to herself she cries,
"Oh misery! Oh misery!
Oh woe is me, oh misery!"

For oft there sits between the heap
That's like an infant's grave in size
And that same pond of which I spoke,
A woman in a scarlet cloak . . .

The Thorn, Sir George Beaumont, 1753–1827 (Richard Wordsworth).

At all times of the day and night
This wretched woman thither goes,
And she is known to every star,
And every wind that blows.
And there beside the thorn she sits
When the blue daylight's in the skies,
And when the whirlwind's on the hill,
Or frosty air is keen and still,
And to herself she cries,
"Oh misery! Oh misery!
Oh woe is me, oh misery!" '

'Now wherefore thus, by day and night,
In rain, in tempest, and in snow,
Thus to the dreary mountain-top
Does this poor woman go?
And why sits she beside the thorn
When the blue daylight's in the sky,
Or when the whirlwind's on the hill,
Or frosty air is keen and still,
And wherefore does she cry –
Oh wherefore, wherefore, tell me why,
Does she repeat that doleful cry?'

'I cannot tell, I wish I could,
For the true reason no one knows;
But if you'd gladly view the spot,
The spot to which she goes –
The heap that's like an infant's grave,
The pond and thorn, so old and grey –
Pass by her door ('tis seldom shut)
And if you see her in her hut,
Then to the spot away!
I never heard of such as dare
Approach the spot when she is there.'

'But wherefore to the mountain-top
Can this unhappy woman go,
Whatever star is in the skies,
Whatever wind may blow?'
'Nay, rack your brain, 'tis all in vain!
I'll tell you everything I know –
But to the thorn, and to the pond
Which is a little step beyond,
I wish that you would go:
Perhaps when you are at the place
You something of her tale may trace.

I'll give you the best help I can:
Before you up the mountain go,
Up to the dreary mountain-top,
I'll tell you all I know.
'Tis now some two-and-twenty years
Since she (her name is Martha Ray)
Gave with a maiden's true good will
Her company to Stephen Hill,
And she was blithe and gay –
And she was happy, happy still
Whene'er she thought of Stephen Hill.

And they had fixed the wedding-day,
The morning that must wed them both;
But Stephen to another maid
Had sworn another oath,
And with this other maid to church
Unthinking Stephen went.
Poor Martha, on that woeful day
A cruel, cruel fire, they say,
Into her bones was sent –
It dried her body like a cinder,
And almost turned her brain to tinder!

They say, full six months after this,
While yet the summer-leaves were green,
She to the mountain-top would go,
And there was often seen.
'Tis said a child was in her womb
(As now to any eye was plain) –
She was with child and she was mad.
Yet often she was sober sad
From her exceeding pain:
Oh me, ten thousand times I'd rather
That he had died, that cruel father!

Sad case for such a brain to hold
Communion with a stirring child –
Sad case, as you may think, for one
Who had a brain so wild!
Last Christmas, when we talked of this,
Old Farmer Simpson did maintain
That in her womb the infant wrought
About its mother's heart, and brought
Her senses back again;
And when at last her time drew near,
Her looks were calm, her senses clear.

No more I know, I wish I did
(And I would tell it all to you),
For what became of this poor child
There's none that ever knew;
And if a child was born or no,
There's no one that could ever tell;
And if 'twas born alive or dead,
There's no one knows, as I have said –
But some remember well
That Martha Ray about this time
Would up the mountain often climb.

And all that winter, when at night
The wind blew from the mountain-peak,
'Twas worth your while, though in the dark,
The churchyard-path to seek;
For many a time and oft were heard
Cries coming from the mountain-head.
Some plainly living voices were,
And others (I've heard many swear)
Were voices of the dead –
I cannot think, whate'er they say,
They had to do with Martha Ray.

But that she goes to this old thorn,
The thorn which I've described to you,
And there sits in a scarlet cloak,
I will be sworn is true.
For one day with my telescope,
To view the ocean wide and bright
(When to this country first I came,
Ere I had heard of Martha's name),
I climbed the mountain's height;
A storm came on, and I could see
No object higher than my knee.

'Twas mist and rain, and storm and rain!
No screen, no fence, could I discover –
And then the wind, in faith it was
A wind full ten times over!
I looked around, I thought I saw
A jutting crag, and off I ran
Head-foremost through the driving rain
The shelter of the crag to gain,
And, as I am a man,
Instead of jutting crag I found
A woman seated on the ground.

I did not speak – I saw her face –
Her face it was enough for me!
I turned about and heard her cry,
"O misery! O misery!"
And there she sits, until the moon
Through half the clear blue sky will go;
And when the little breezes make
The waters of the pond to shake
(As all the country know),
She shudders, and you hear her cry,
"Oh misery! Oh misery!" '

'But what's the thorn, and what's the pond,
And what's the hill of moss to her?
And what's the creeping breeze that comes
The little pond to stir?'
'I cannot tell, but some will say
She hanged her baby on the tree;
Some say she drowned it in the pond,
Which is a little step beyond;
But each and all agree
The little babe was buried there,
Beneath that hill of moss so fair.

I've heard the scarlet moss is red
With drops of that poor infant's blood –
But kill a new-born infant thus,
I do not think she could!
Some say, if to the pond you go
And fix on it a steady view,
The shadow of a babe you trace,
A baby and a baby's face,
And that it looks at you –
Whene'er you look on it, 'tis plain
The baby looks at you again.

And some had sworn an oath that she
Should be to public justice brought;
And for the little infant's bones
With spades they would have sought.
But then the beauteous hill of moss
Before their eyes began to stir,
And for full fifty yards around
The grass it shook upon the ground –
But all do still aver
The little babe is buried there,
Beneath that hill of moss so fair.

I cannot tell how this may be,
But plain it is the thorn is bound
With heavy tufts of moss that strive
To drag it to the ground.
And this I know, full many a time
When she was on the mountain high,
By day, and in the silent night
When all the stars shone clear and bright,
That I have heard her cry,
"Oh misery! Oh misery!
O woe is me, oh misery!" '

The Idiot Boy

'Tis eight o'clock, a clear March night,
The moon is up, the sky is blue,
The owlet in the moonlight air
He shouts from nobody knows where,
He lengthens out his lonely shout,
Halloo! halloo! a long halloo!

Why bustle thus about your door?
What means this bustle, Betty Foy?
Why are you in this mighty fret,
And why on horseback have you set
Him whom you love, your idiot boy?

Beneath the moon that shines so bright,
Till she is tired, let Betty Foy
With girt and stirrup fiddle-faddle –
But wherefore set upon a saddle
Him whom she loves, her idiot boy?

There's scarce a soul that's out of bed;
Good Betty, put him down again!
His lips with joy they burr at you,
But Betty, what has he to do
With stirrup, saddle, or with rein?

The world will say 'tis very idle –
Bethink you of the time of night!
There's not a mother, no not one,
But when she hears what you have done,
Oh Betty she'll be in a fright!

But Betty's bent on her intent,
For her good neighbour, Susan Gale
(Old Susan, she who dwells alone),
Is sick, and makes a piteous moan
As if her very life would fail.

There's not a house within a mile,
No hand to help them in distress;
Old Susan lies abed in pain,
And sorely puzzled are the twain,
For what she ails they cannot guess.

And Betty's husband's at the wood
Where by the week he doth abide,
A woodman in the distant vale;
There's none to help poor Susan Gale –
What must be done, what will betide?

And Betty from the lane has fetched
Her pony (that is mild and good
Whether he be in joy or pain,
Feeding at will along the lane
Or bringing faggots from the wood),

And he is all in travelling trim.
And by the moonlight Betty Foy
Has up upon the saddle set
(The like was never heard of yet!)
Him whom she loves, her idiot boy.

And he must post without delay
Across the bridge that's in the dale,
And by the church, and o'er the down,
To bring a doctor from the town,
Or she will die, old Susan Gale.

There is no need of boot or spur,
There is no need of whip or wand,
For Johnny has his holly-bough,
And with a hurly-burly now
He shakes the green bough in his hand.

And Betty o'er and o'er has told
The boy who is her best delight,
Both what to follow, what to shun,
What do, and what to leave undone,
How turn to left, and how to right.

And Betty's most especial charge
Was, 'Johnny! Johnny! mind that you
Come home again, nor stop at all,
Come home again, whate'er befall,
My Johnny do, I pray you do.'

To this did Johnny answer make
Both with his head and with his hand,
And proudly shook the bridle too;
And then, his words were not a few,
Which Betty well could understand!

And now that Johnny is just going,
Though Betty's in a mighty flurry,
She gently pats the pony's side
On which her idiot boy must ride,
And seems no longer in a hurry.

But when the pony moved his legs,
Oh, then for the poor idiot boy! –
For joy he cannot hold the bridle,
For joy his head and heels are idle,
He's idle all for very joy!

And while the pony moves his legs,
In Johnny's left-hand you may see
The green bough's motionless and dead;
The moon that shines above his head
Is not more still and mute than he.

His heart it was so full of glee
That till full fifty yards were gone
He quite forgot his holly whip
And all his skill in horsemanship –
Oh, happy, happy, happy John!

And Betty's standing at the door,
And Betty's face with joy o'erflows:
Proud of herself, and proud of him,
She sees him in his travelling trim,
How quietly her Johnny goes.

The silence of her idiot boy,
What hopes it sends to Betty's heart!
He's at the guide-post – he turns right –
She watches till he's out of sight,
And Betty will not then depart.

Burr, burr, now Johnny's lips they burr,
As loud as any mill, or near it!
Meek as a lamb the pony moves,
And Johnny makes the noise he loves,
And Betty listens, glad to hear it.

Away she hies to Susan Gale,
And Johnny's in a merry tune;
The owlets hoot, the owlets curr,
And Johnny's lips they burr, burr, burr,
And on he goes beneath the moon.

The owlet in the moonlight air
He shouts from nobody knows where,
He lengthens out his lonely shout,
Halloo! halloo! a long halloo!

Thomas Bewick, engraving for *British Birds*, 1797 (Iain Bain).

His steed and he right well agree,
For of this pony there's a rumour
That should he lose his eyes and ears,
And should he live a thousand years,
He never will be out of humour.

But then he is a horse that thinks,
And when he thinks his pace is slack!
Now, though he knows poor Johnny well,
Yet for his life he cannot tell
What he has got upon his back.

So through the moonlight lanes they go,
And far into the moonlight dale,
And by the church, and o'er the down,
To bring a doctor from the town,
To comfort poor old Susan Gale.

And Betty, now at Susan's side,
Is in the middle of her story,
What comfort Johnny soon will bring –
With many a most diverting thing
Of Johnny's wit and Johnny's glory.

And Betty's still at Susan's side
(By this time she's not quite so flurried);
Demure with porringer and plate
She sits, as if in Susan's fate
Her life and soul were buried.

But Betty, poor good woman, she
(You plainly in her face may read it)
Could lend out of that moment's store
Five years of happiness or more,
To any that might need it.

But yet I guess that now and then
With Betty all was not so well;
And to the road she turns her ears,
And thence full many a sound she hears
Which she to Susan will not tell.

Poor Susan moans, poor Susan groans,
'As sure as there's a moon in heaven',
Cries Betty, 'he'll be back again!
They'll both be here, 'tis almost ten –
They'll both be here before eleven.'

Poor Susan moans, poor Susan groans,
The clock gives warning for eleven –
'Tis on the stroke! 'If Johnny's near',
Quoth Betty, 'he will soon be here,
As sure as there's a moon in heaven.'

The clock is on the stroke of twelve
And Johnny is not yet in sight;
The moon's in heaven, as Betty sees,
But Betty is not quite at ease –
And Susan has a dreadful night!

And Betty, half an hour ago,
On Johnny vile reflections cast
('A little idle sauntering thing' –
With other names, an endless string),
But now that time is gone and past.

And Betty's drooping at the heart,
That happy time all past and gone:
'How can it be he is so late?
The doctor he has made him wait –
Susan, they'll both be here anon.'

And Susan's growing worse and worse,
And Betty's in a sad quandry –
And then there's nobody to say
If she must go or she must stay –
She's in a sad quandry.

The clock is on the stroke of one,
But neither doctor nor his guide
Appear along the moonlight road;
There's neither horse nor man abroad,
And Betty's still at Susan's side.

And Susan she begins to fear
Of sad mischances not a few:
That Johnny may perhaps be drowned,
Or lost perhaps, and never found –
Which they must both for ever rue.

She prefaced half a hint of this
With, 'God forbid it should be true!'
At the first word that Susan said
Cried Betty – rising from the bed –
'Susan, I'd gladly stay with you!

I must be gone, I must away!
Consider, Johnny's but half wise;
Susan, we must take care of him.
If he is hurt in life or limb – '
'Oh God forbid!' poor Susan cries.

'What can I do?' says Betty, going,
'What can I do to ease your pain?
Good Susan tell me, and I'll stay;
I fear you're in a dreadful way,
But I shall soon be back again.'

'Good Betty go, good Betty go,
There's nothing that can ease my pain!'
Then off she hies, but with a prayer
That God poor Susan's life would spare,
Till she comes back again.

So through the moonlight lane she goes,
And far into the moonlight dale;
And how she ran, and how she walked,
And all that to herself she talked,
Would surely be a tedious tale.

In high and low, above, below,
In great and small, in round and square,
In tree and tower, was Johnny seen –
In bush and brake, in black and green,
'Twas Johnny, Johnny, everywhere.

She's past the bridge that's in the dale,
And now the thought torments her sore,
Johnny perhaps his horse forsook
To hunt the moon that's in the brook,
And never will be heard of more.

And now she's high upon the down,
Alone amid a prospect wide;
There's neither Johnny nor his horse
Among the fern or in the gorse;
There's neither doctor nor his guide.

'Oh saints, what is become of him?
Perhaps he's climbed into an oak,
Where he will stay till he is dead;
Or sadly he has been misled,
And joined the wandering gypsy-folk.

Or him that wicked pony's carried
To the dark cave, the goblin's hall,
Or in the castle he's pursuing,
Among the ghosts, his own undoing;
Or playing with the waterfall.'

At poor old Susan then she railed
While to the town she posts away,
'If Susan had not been so ill,
Alas, I should have had him still,
My Johnny, till my dying day.'

Poor Betty, in this sad distemper,
The doctor's self would hardly spare;
Unworthy things she talked and wild!
Even he (of cattle the most mild),
The pony had his share.

And now she's got into the town,
And to the doctor's door she hies;
'Tis silence all on every side –
The town so long, the town so wide,
Is silent as the skies.

And now she's at the doctor's door,
She lifts the knocker, rap, rap, rap;
The doctor at the casement shows
His glimmering eyes that peep and doze,
And one hand rubs his old nightcap.

'Oh doctor, doctor, where's my Johnny?'
'I'm here, what is't you want with me?'
'Oh sir, you know I'm Betty Foy,
And I have lost my poor dear boy!
You know him, him you often see –

He's not so wise as some folks be.'
'The devil take his wisdom!' said
The doctor, looking somewhat grim;
'What, woman, should I know of him?'
And, grumbling, he went back to bed.

'O woe is me! O woe is me!
Here will I die, here will I die;
I thought to find my Johnny here,
But he is neither far nor near –
Oh what a wretched mother I!'

She stops, she stands, she looks about,
Which way to turn she cannot tell.
Poor Betty! It would ease her pain
If she had heart to knock again;
The clock strikes three – a dismal knell!

Then up along the town she hies,
No wonder if her senses fail,
This piteous news so much it shocked her,
She quite forgot to send the doctor,
To comfort poor old Susan Gale.

And now she's high upon the down,
And she can see a mile of road,
'Oh cruel, I'm almost three-score!
Such night as this was ne'er before,
There's not a single soul abroad.'

She listens, but she cannot hear
The foot of horse, the voice of man;
The streams with softest sound are flowing,
The grass you almost hear it growing –
You hear it now if e'er you can.

The owlets through the long blue night
Are shouting to each other still:
Fond lovers, yet not quite hob-nob,
They lengthen out the tremulous sob
That echoes far from hill to hill.

Poor Betty now has lost all hope,
Her thoughts are bent on deadly sin;
A green-grown pond she just has passed,
And from the brink she hurries fast,
Lest she should drown herself therein.

And now she sits her down and weeps
(Such tears she never shed before),
'Oh dear, dear pony! My sweet joy!
Oh carry back my idiot boy,
And we will ne'er o'erload thee more!'

A thought is come into her head:
'The pony he is mild and good,
And we have always used him well;
Perhaps he's gone along the dell
And carried Johnny to the wood.'

Then up she springs as if on wings,
She thinks no more of deadly sin –
If Betty fifty ponds should see,
The last of all her thoughts would be
To drown herself therein.

Oh reader, now that I might tell
What Johnny and his horse are doing!
What they've been doing all this time –
Oh could I put it into rhyme,
A most delightful tale pursuing!

117

So through the moonlight lane she goes,
And far into the moonlight dale . . .

Shepherds under a Full Moon, Samuel Palmer, c. 1830 (Ashmolean Museum, Oxford).

Perhaps – and no unlikely thought –
He with his pony now doth roam
The cliffs and peaks so high that are,
To lay his hands upon a star,
And in his pocket bring it home.

Perhaps he's turned himself about,
His face unto his horse's tail,
And still and mute, in wonder lost,
All like a silent horseman-ghost
He travels on along the vale.

And now perhaps he's hunting sheep,
A fierce and dreadful hunter he!
Yon valley, that's so trim and green,
In five months' time, should he be seen,
A desert wilderness will be.

Perhaps, with head and heels on fire
And like the very soul of evil,
He's galloping away, away,
And so he'll gallop on for aye,
The bane of all that dread the devil.

I to the muses have been bound
These fourteen years by strong indentures;
Oh gentle muses, let me tell
But half of what to him befell,
For sure he met with strange adventures!

Oh gentle muses, is this kind?
Why will ye thus my suit repel?
Why of your further aid bereave me?
And can ye thus unfriended leave me,
Ye muses, whom I love so well?

Who's yon, that near the waterfall
(Which thunders down with headlong force
Beneath the moon – yet shining fair)
As careless as if nothing were,
Sits upright on a feeding horse?

Unto his horse, that's feeding free,
He seems, I think, the rein to give;
Of moon or stars he takes no heed
(Of such we in romances read) –
'Tis Johnny, Johnny, as I live!

And that's the very pony too!
Where is she, where is Betty Foy?
She hardly can sustain her fears –
The roaring waterfall she hears,
And cannot find her idiot boy.

Your pony's worth his weight in gold;
Then calm your terrors, Betty Foy! –
She's coming from among the trees,
And now, all full in view, she sees
Him whom she loves, her idiot boy.

And Betty sees the pony too!
Why stand you thus good Betty Foy?
It is no goblin, 'tis no ghost,
'Tis he whom you so long have lost,
He whom you love, your idiot boy.

She looks again – her arms are up –
She screams – she cannot move for joy!
She darts as with a torrent's force,
She almost has o'erturned the horse,
And fast she holds her idiot boy.

And Johnny burrs and laughs aloud –
Whether in cunning or in joy
I cannot tell, but while he laughs
Betty a drunken pleasure quaffs
To hear again her idiot boy.

And now she's at the pony's tail,
And now she's at the pony's head,
On that side now, and now on this;
And, almost stifled with her bliss,
A few sad tears does Betty shed.

She kisses o'er and o'er again
Him whom she loves, her idiot boy;
She's happy here, she's happy there,
She is uneasy everywhere –
Her limbs are all alive with joy.

She pats the pony, where or when
She knows not, happy Betty Foy!
The little pony glad may be,
But he is milder far than she,
You hardly can perceive his joy.

'Oh Johnny, never mind the doctor!
You've done your best, and that is all.'
She took the reins, when this was said,
And gently turned the pony's head
From the loud waterfall.

By this the stars were almost gone;
The moon was setting on the hill,
So pale you scarcely looked at her;
The little birds began to stir,
Though yet their tongues were still.

The pony, Betty, and her boy,
Wind slowly through the woody dale:
And who is she, betimes abroad,
That hobbles up the steep rough road –
Who is it, but old Susan Gale?

Long Susan lay deep lost in thought,
And many dreadful fears beset her,
Both for her messenger and nurse;
And as her mind grew worse and worse,
Her body it grew better.

She turned, she tossed herself in bed,
On all sides doubts and terrors met her!
Point after point did she discuss –
And while her mind was fighting thus,
Her body still grew better.

'Alas, what is become of them?
These fears can never be endured –
I'll to the wood.' The word scarce said,
Did Susan rise up from her bed,
As if by magic cured.

Away she posts up hill and down,
And to the wood at length is come;
She spies her friends, she shouts a greeting –
Oh me, it is a merry meeting
As ever was in Christendom!

The owls have hardly sung their last
While our four travellers homeward wend;
The owls have hooted all night long –
And with the owls began my song,
And with the owls must end.

For while they all were travelling home,
Cried Betty, 'Tell us Johnny, do,
Where all this long night you have been,
What you have heard, what you have seen –
And Johnny, mind you tell us true.'

Now Johnny all night long had heard
The owls in tuneful concert strive;
No doubt too he the moon had seen,
For in the moonlight he had been
From eight o'clock till five.

And thus to Betty's question, he
Made answer, like a traveller bold
(His very words I give to you):
'The cocks did crow to-whoo, to-whoo,
And the sun did shine so cold.'
Thus answered Johnny in his glory,
And that was all his travel's story.

Lines Written in Early Spring

I heard a thousand blended notes
While in a grove I sat reclined,
In that sweet mood when pleasant thoughts
Bring sad thoughts to the mind.

To her fair works did Nature link
The human soul that through me ran,
And much it grieved my heart to think
What man has made of man.

Through primrose-tufts, in that sweet bower,
The periwinkle trailed its wreathes;
And 'tis my faith that every flower
Enjoys the air it breathes.

The birds around me hopped and played,
Their thoughts I cannot measure,
But the least motion which they made,
It seemed a thrill of pleasure.

The budding twigs spread out their fan,
To catch the breezy air;
And I must think – do all I can –
That there was pleasure there.

If I these thoughts may not prevent,
If such be of my creed the plan,
Have I not reason to lament
What man has made of man?

We Are Seven

A simple child, dear brother Jim,
That lightly draws its breath,
And feels its life in every limb,
What should it know of death?

I met a little cottage-girl
(She was eight years old, she said),
Her hair was thick with many a curl
That clustered round her head.

She had a rustic, woodland air,
And she was wildly clad;
Her eyes were fair, and very fair –
Her beauty made me glad.

'Sisters and brothers, little maid,
How many may you be?'
'How many? Seven in all', she said,
And wondering looked at me.

'And where are they, I pray you tell?'
She answered, 'Seven are we,
And two of us at Conway dwell,
And two are gone to sea;

Two of us in the churchyard lie,
My sister and my brother;
And in the churchyard-cottage, I
Dwell near them with my mother.'

'You say that two at Conway dwell,
And two are gone to sea,
Yet you are seven – I pray you tell,
Sweet maid, how this may be?'

Whene'er I take my walks abroad,
How many poor I see!
What shall I render to my God
For all his gifts to me?

THE

LITTLE MAID

AND

The Gentleman;

OR,

WE ARE SEVEN.

EMBELLISHED WITH ENGRAVINGS.

YORK:
Printed by J. Kendrew, 23, Colliergate.

6

I met a little cottage girl,
  She was eight years old she said;
Her hair was thick with many a curl
  That cluster'd round her head.

She had a rustic woodland air,
  And she was wildly clad;
Her eyes were fair, and very fair,
  Her beauty made me glad.

7

" Sisters and brothers, little maid,
  " How many may you be;"
" How many; seven in all," she said,
  And wond'ring look'd at me.

"And where are they, I pray you tell,
  She answered "seven are we,
" And two of us at Conway dwell,
  ' And two are gone to sea.

The Little Maid and the Gentleman, rare chapbook version of *We Are Seven*, $3\frac{3}{4} \times 2\frac{1}{2}$ inches, for sale to the wider audience whom the poet especially hoped to reach (Jonathan Wordsworth).

Then did the little maid reply,
'Seven boys and girls are we –
Two of us in the churchyard lie,
Beneath the churchyard-tree.'

'You run about, my little maid,
Your limbs they are alive;
If two are in the churchyard laid,
Then ye are only five.'

'Their graves are green, they may be seen',
The little maid replied,
'Twelve steps or more from my mother's door,
And they are side by side.

My stockings there I often knit,
My kerchief there I hem,
And there upon the ground I sit,
I sit and sing to them.

And often after sunset, sir,
When it is light and fair,
I take my little porringer
And eat my supper there.

The first that died was little Jane,
In bed she moaning lay
Till God released her of her pain,
And then she went away.

So in the churchyard she was laid,
And all the summer dry
Together round her grave we played –
My brother John and I.

And when the ground was white with snow
And I could run and slide,
My brother John was forced to go,
And he lies by her side.'

'How many are you then', said I,
'If they two are in heaven?'
The little maiden did reply,
'O master, we are seven!'

'But they are dead, those two are dead –
Their spirits are in heaven!'
'Twas throwing words away, for still
The little maid would have her will,
And said, 'Nay, we are seven!'

Tintern Abbey

Five years have passed – five summers, with the length
Of five long winters – and again I hear
These waters rolling from their mountain-springs
With a sweet inland murmur. Once again
Do I behold these steep and lofty cliffs,
Which on a wild secluded scene impress
Thoughts of more deep seclusion, and connect
The landscape with the quiet of the sky.
The day is come when I again repose
Here under this dark sycamore, and view
These plots of cottage-ground, these orchard-tufts
Which at this season, with their unripe fruits,
Among the woods and copses lose themselves,
Nor with their green and simple hue disturb
The wild green landscape. Once again I see
These hedge-rows (hardly hedge-rows, little lines
Of sportive wood run wild), these pastoral farms
Green to the very door, and wreathes of smoke
Sent up in silence from among the trees
With some uncertain notice, as might seem,
Of vagrant dwellers in the houseless woods,
Or of some hermit's cave, where by his fire
The hermit sits alone.
                              Though absent long,
These forms of beauty have not been to me
As is a landscape to a blind man's eye;
But oft, in lonely rooms, and mid the din
Of towns and cities, I have owed to them
In hours of weariness sensations sweet
Felt in the blood, and felt along the heart,
And passing even into my purer mind
With tranquil restoration – feelings too
Of unremembered pleasure: such, perhaps,
As may have had no trivial influence

On that best portion of a good man's life,
His little nameless unremembered acts
Of kindness and of love.
                                    Nor less, I trust,
To them I may have owed another gift,
Of aspect more sublime : that blessed mood
In which the burden of the mystery,
In which the heavy and the weary weight
Of all this unintelligible world,
Is lightened – that serene and blessed mood
In which the affections gently lead us on,
Until, the breath of this corporeal frame
And even the motion of our human blood
Almost suspended, we are laid asleep
In body and become a living soul,
While, with an eye made quiet by the power
Of harmony and the deep power of joy,
We see into the life of things.
                                        If this
Be but a vain belief, yet oh, how oft
In darkness and amid the many shapes
Of joyless daylight, when the fretful stir
Unprofitable and the fever of the world
Have hung upon the beatings of my heart,
How oft in spirit have I turned to thee
O sylvan Wye – thou wanderer through the woods –
How often has my spirit turned to thee!
   And now, with gleams of half-extinguished thought,
With many recognitions dim and faint,
And somewhat of a sad perplexity,
The picture of the mind revives again,
While here I stand, not only with the sense
Of present pleasure, but with pleasing thoughts
That in this moment there is life and food
For future years. And so I dare to hope
Though changed, no doubt, from what I was when first
I came among these hills, when like a roe

I bounded o'er the mountains, by the sides
Of the deep rivers and the lonely streams,
Wherever Nature led – more like a man
Flying from something that he dreads, than one
Who sought the thing he loved. For Nature then
(The coarser pleasures of my boyish days,
And their glad animal movements, all gone by)
To me was all in all.
                      I cannot paint
What then I was: the sounding cataract
Haunted me like a passion; the tall rock,
The mountain, and the deep and gloomy wood,
Their colours and their forms, were then to me
An appetite – a feeling and a love
That had no need of a remoter charm
By thought supplied, or any interest
Unborrowed from the eye.
                        That time is past,
And all its aching joys are now no more,
And all its dizzy raptures. Not for this
Faint I, nor mourn, nor murmur: other gifts
Have followed, for such loss, I would believe,
Abundant recompense. For I have learned
To look on Nature not as in the hour
Of thoughtless youth, but hearing oftentimes
The still, sad music of humanity,
Nor harsh, nor grating, though of ample power
To chasten and subdue. And I have felt
A presence that disturbs me with the joy
Of elevated thoughts, a sense sublime
Of something far more deeply interfused,
Whose dwelling is the light of setting suns,
And the round ocean, and the living air,
And the blue sky, and in the mind of man –
A motion and a spirit that impels
All thinking things, all objects of all thought,
And rolls through all things.

Therefore am I still
A lover of the meadows and the woods
And mountains, and of all that we behold
From this green earth – of all the mighty world
Of eye and ear, both what they half-create,
And what perceive – well pleased to recognise
In Nature and the language of the sense
The anchor of my purest thoughts, the nurse,
The guide, the guardian of my heart, and soul
Of all my moral being.
                            Nor perchance
If I were not thus taught, should I the more
Suffer my genial spirits to decay;
For thou art with me, here upon the banks
Of this fair river, thou, my dearest friend,
My dear, dear friend, and in thy voice I catch
The language of my former heart – and read
My former pleasures in the shooting lights
Of thy wild eyes. Oh, yet a little while
May I behold in thee what I was once,
My dear, dear sister! And this prayer I make,
Knowing that Nature never did betray
The heart that loved her: 'tis her privilege
Through all the years of this our life to lead
From joy to joy, for she can so inform
The mind that is within us, so impress
With quietness and beauty, and so feed
With lofty thoughts, that neither evil tongues,
Rash judgements, nor the sneers of selfish men,
Nor greetings where no kindness is, nor all
The dreary intercourse of daily life,
Shall e'er prevail against us, or disturb
Our cheerful faith that all which we behold
Is full of blessings.
                            Therefore let the moon
Shine on thee in thy solitary walk,
And let the misty mountain-winds be free

To blow against thee; and in after years,
When these wild ecstasies shall be matured
Into a sober pleasure, when thy mind
Shall be a mansion for all lovely forms,
Thy memory be as a dwelling-place
For all sweet sounds and harmonies, oh, then
If solitude, or fear, or pain, or grief,
Should be thy portion, with what healing thoughts
Of tender joy wilt thou remember me
And these my exhortations!
                        Nor perchance
If I should be where I no more can hear
Thy voice, nor catch from thy wild eyes these gleams
Of past existence, wilt thou then forget
That on the banks of this delightful stream
We stood together, and that I, so long
A worshipper of Nature, hither came
Unwearied in that service – rather say
With warmer love, oh, with far deeper zeal
Of holier love. Nor wilt thou then forget
That after many wanderings, many years
Of absence, these steep woods and lofty cliffs,
And this green pastoral landscape, were to me
More dear, both for themselves, and for thy sake.

Lucy Gray

Oft had I heard of Lucy Gray,
And when I crossed the wild
I chanced to see at break of day
The solitary child.

No mate, no comrade, Lucy knew;
She dwelt on a wide moor,
The sweetest thing that ever grew
Beside a human door!

Yet you may spy the fawn at play,
The hare upon the green,
But the sweet face of Lucy Gray
Will never more be seen.

'Tonight will be a stormy night,
You to the town must go,
And take a lantern, child, to light
Your mother through the snow.'

'That, father, will I gladly do,
'Tis scarcely afternoon –
The minster-clock has just struck two,
And yonder is the moon!'

At this the father raised his hook
And snapped a faggot-band;
He plied his work, and Lucy took
The lantern in her hand.

Not blither is the mountain-roe:
With many a wanton stroke
Her feet disperse the powdery snow
That rises up like smoke.

Once again
Do I behold these steep and lofty cliffs,
Which on a wild secluded scene impress
Thoughts of more deep seclusion, and connect
The landscape with the quiet of the sky.

Tintern Abbey, aquatint frontispiece by Theodore Henry Fielding
in *A Picturesque Description of The River Wye*, 1819.

The storm came on before its time;
She wandered up and down,
And many a hill did Lucy climb
But never reached the town.

The wretched parents all that night
Went shouting far and wide,
But there was neither sound nor sight
To serve them for a guide.

At daybreak on a hill they stood
That overlooked the moor,
And thence they saw the bridge of wood
A furlong from their door.

And now they homeward turned, and cried,
'In heaven we all shall meet' –
When in the snow the mother spied
The print of Lucy's feet.

Then downward from the steep hill's edge
They tracked the footmarks small,
And through the broken hawthorn-hedge,
And by the long stone wall.

And then an open field they crossed –
The marks were still the same –
They tracked them on, nor ever lost,
And to the bridge they came.

They followed from the snowy bank
The footmarks one by one,
Into the middle of the plank,
And further there were none.

Yet some maintain that to this day
She is a living child,
That you may see sweet Lucy Gray
Upon the lonesome wild.

O'er rough and smooth she trips along
And never looks behind,
And sings a solitary song
That whistles in the wind.

Strange Fits of Passion

Strange fits of passion I have known,
And I will dare to tell,
But in the lover's ear alone,
What once to me befell.

When she I loved was strong and gay
And like a rose in June,
I to her cottage bent my way
Beneath the evening moon.

Upon the moon I fixed my eye
All over the wide lea;
My horse trudged on, and we drew nigh
Those paths so dear to me.

And now we reached the orchard-plot,
And as we climbed the hill,
Towards the roof of Lucy's cot
The moon descended still.

In one of those sweet dreams I slept,
Kind Nature's gentlest boon,
And all the while my eyes I kept
On the descending moon.

My horse moved on – hoof after hoof
He raised and never stopped –
When down behind the cottage-roof
At once the planet dropped.

What fond and wayward thoughts will slide
Into a lover's head:
'O mercy', to myself I cried,
'If Lucy should be dead!'

She Dwelt Among the Untrodden Ways

She dwelt among the untrodden ways
    Beside the springs of Dove,
A maid whom there were none to praise
    And very few to love –

A violet by a mossy stone
    Half hidden from the eye,
Fair as a star when only one
    Is shining in the sky.

She *lived* unknown, and few could know
    When Lucy ceased to be;
But she is in her grave, and oh
    The difference to me!

A Slumber Did My Spirit Seal

A slumber did my spirit seal –
I had no human fears –
She seemed a thing that could not feel
The touch of earthly years.

No motion has she now, no force,
She neither hears nor sees,
Rolled round in earth's diurnal course
With rocks and stones and trees.

Three Years She Grew

Three years she grew in sun and shower,
Then Nature said: 'A lovelier flower
On earth was never sown –
This child I to myself will take,
She shall be mine, and I will make
A lady of my own.

Myself will to my darling be
Both law and impulse, and with me
The girl – in rock and plain,
In earth and heaven, in glade and bower –
Shall feel an overseeing power
To kindle or restrain.

She shall be sportive as the fawn
That wild with glee across the lawn
Or up the mountain springs;
And hers shall be the breathing balm,
And hers the silence and the calm,
Of mute insensate things.

The floating clouds their state shall lend
To her, for her the willow bend;
Nor shall she fail to see
Even in the motions of the storm
A beauty that shall mould her form
By silent sympathy.

The stars of midnight shall be dear
To her, and she shall lean her ear
In many a secret place
Where rivulets dance their wayward round,
And beauty born of murmuring sound
Shall pass into her face.

And vital feelings of delight
Shall rear her form to stately height,
Her virgin bosom swell –
Such thoughts to Lucy I will give
While she and I together live
Here in this happy dell.'

Thus Nature spake: the work was done.
How soon my Lucy's race was run!
She died – and left to me
This heath, this calm and quiet scene,
The memory of what has been
And never more will be.

Two April Mornings

We walked along while bright and red
Uprose the morning sun,
And Matthew stopped – he looked, and said
'The will of God be done!'

A village schoolmaster was he
With hair of glittering grey,
As blithe a man as you could see
On a spring holiday.

And on that morning, through the grass
And by the steaming rills,
We travelled merrily to pass
A day among the hills.

'Our work', said I, 'was well begun –
Then, from thy breast what thought,
Beneath so beautiful a sun,
So sad a sigh has brought?'

A second time did Matthew stop
And, fixing still his eye
Upon the eastern mountain-top,
To me he made reply:

'Yon cloud with that long purple cleft
Brings fresh into my mind
A day like this which I have left
Full thirty years behind.

And on that slope of springing corn
The self-same crimson hue
Fell from the sky that April morn –
The same which now I view.

With rod and line my silent sport
I plied by Derwent's wave,
And, coming to the church, stopped short
Beside my daughter's grave.

Nine summers had she scarcely seen,
The pride of all the vale!
And then she sang – she would have been
A very nightingale!

Six feet in earth my Emma lay,
And yet I loved her more
(For so it seemed) than till that day
I e'er had loved before.

And, turning from her grave, I met
Beside the churchyard-yew
A blooming girl, whose hair was wet
With points of morning dew.

A basket on her head she bare,
Her brow was smooth and white,
To see a child so very fair,
It was a pure delight!

No fountain from its rocky cave
E'er tripped with foot so free;
She seemed as happy as a wave
That dances on the sea.

There came from me a sigh of pain
Which I could ill confine;
I looked at her, and looked again –
And did not wish her mine.'

Matthew is in his grave, yet now
Methinks I see him stand,
As at that moment, with his bough
Of wilding in his hand.

The Fountain

We talked with open heart, and tongue
Affectionate and true –
A pair of friends, though I was young,
And Matthew seventy-two.

We lay beneath a spreading oak,
Beside a mossy seat,
And from the turf a fountain broke
And gurgled at our feet.

Now, Matthew, let us try to match
This water's pleasant tune
With some old Border song or catch
That suits a summer's noon.

Or of the church-clock and the chimes
Sing here beneath the shade,
That half-mad thing of witty rhymes
Which you last April made!

In silence Matthew lay, and eyed
The spring beneath the tree;
And thus the dear old man replied,
The grey-haired man of glee:

'Down to the vale this water steers –
How merrily it goes! –
'Twill murmur on a thousand years,
And flow as now it flows.

And here, on this delightful day,
I cannot choose but think
How oft, a vigorous man, I lay
Beside this fountain's brink.

My eyes are dim with childish tears,
My heart is idly stirred,
For the same sound is in my ears
Which in those days I heard.

Thus fares it still in our decay;
And yet the wiser mind
Mourns less for what age takes away
Than what it leaves behind.

The blackbird in the summer trees,
The lark upon the hill,
Let loose their carols when they please,
Are quiet when they will.

With Nature never do they wage
A foolish strife; they see
A happy youth, and their old age
Is beautiful and free.

But we are pressed by heavy laws,
And often – glad no more –
We wear a face of joy, because
We have been glad of yore.

If there is one who need bemoan
His kindred laid in earth,
The household-hearts that were his own,
It is the man of mirth.

My days, my friend, are almost gone,
My life has been approved,
And many love me, but by none
Am I enough beloved.'

'Now both himself and me he wrongs,
The man who thus complains!
I live and sing my idle songs
Upon these happy plains –

And, Matthew, for thy children dead
I'll be a son to thee!'
At this he grasped his hands, and said
'Alas, that cannot be!'

We rose up from the fountain-side,
And down the smooth descent
Of the green sheep-track did we glide,
And through the wood we went,

And, ere we came to Leonard's rock,
He sang those witty rhymes
About the crazy old church-clock
And the bewildered chimes.

The Glad Preamble

Oh there is blessing in this gentle breeze,
That blows from the green fields and from the clouds
And from the sky; it beats against my cheek,
And seems half conscious of the joy it gives.
O welcome messenger! O welcome friend!
A captive greets thee, coming from a house
Of bondage, from yon city's walls set free,
A prison where he hath been long immured.
Now I am free, enfranchised and at large,
May fix my habitation where I will.
What dwelling shall receive me, in what vale
Shall be my harbour, underneath what grove
Shall I take up my home, and what sweet stream
Shall with its murmurs lull me to my rest?
The earth is all before me – with a heart
Joyous, nor scared at its own liberty,
I look about, and should the guide I choose
Be nothing better than a wandering cloud
I cannot miss my way.
                    I breathe again –
Trances of thought and mountings of the mind
Come fast upon me. It is shaken off,
As by miraculous gift 'tis shaken off,
That burden of my own unnatural self,
The heavy weight of many a weary day
Not mine, and such as were not made for me.
Long months of peace (if such bold word accord
With any promises of human life),
Long months of ease and undisturbed delight
Are mine in prospect. Whither shall I turn,
By road or pathway, or through open field,
Or shall a twig or any floating thing
Upon the river point me out my course?
  Enough that I am free, for months to come

May dedicate myself to chosen tasks,
May quit the tiresome sea and dwell on shore –
If not a settler on the soil, at least
To drink wild water, and to pluck green herbs,
And gather fruits fresh from their native tree.
Nay more, if I may trust myself, this hour
Hath brought a gift that consecrates my joy;
For I, methought, while the sweet breath of heaven
Was blowing on my body, felt within
A corresponding mild creative breeze,
A vital breeze which travelled gently on
O'er things which it had made, and is become
A tempest, a redundant energy,
Vexing its own creation.
                              'Tis a power
That does not come unrecognised, a storm
Which, breaking up a long-continued frost,
Brings with it vernal promises, the hope
Of active days, of dignity and thought,
Of prowess in an honourable field,
Pure passions, virtue, knowledge, and delight,
The holy life of music and of verse.

(*1805* i, 1–54)

Tribute to Dorothy

                              Mine eyes did ne'er
Rest on a lovely object, nor my mind
Take pleasure in the midst of happy thoughts,
But either she whom now I have, who now
Divides with me this loved abode, was there
Or not far off. Where'er my footsteps turned,
Her voice was like a hidden bird that sang;
The thought of her was like a flash of light
Or an unseen companionship, a breath
Or fragrance independent of the wind . . .

                 (1800 *Home at Grasmere*, 104–13)

Water Fowl

Behold them, how they shape
Orb after orb their course still round and round
Above the area of the lake, their own
Adopted region, girding it about
In wanton repetition, yet therewith –
With that large circle evermore renewed –
Hundreds of curves and circlets, high and low,
Backwards and forwards, progress intricate,
As if one spirit was in all and swayed
Their indefatigable flight.

'Tis done!
Ten times or more I fancied it had ceased,
And lo, the vanished company again
Ascending – list, again I hear their wings –
Faint, faint at first, and then an eager sound,
Passed in a moment, and as faint again.
They tempt the sun to sport among their plumes;
They tempt the water and the gleaming ice
To show them a fair image. 'Tis themselves,
Their own fair forms upon the glimmering plain,
Painted more soft and fair as they descend
Almost to touch, then up again aloft,
Up with a sally and a flash of speed
As if they scorned both resting-place and rest.

Michael

While this good household thus were living on
From day to day, to Michael's ear there came
Distressful tidings. Long before the time
Of which I speak, the shepherd had been bound
In surety for his brother's son, a man
Of an industrious life and ample means,
But unforeseen misfortunes suddenly
Had pressed upon him, and old Michael now
Was summoned to discharge the forfeiture –
A grievous penalty, but little less
Than half his substance. This unlooked-for claim,
At the first hearing, for a moment took
More hope out of his life than he supposed
That any old man ever could have lost.
As soon as he had gathered so much strength
That he could look his trouble in the face,
It seemed that his sole refuge was to sell
A portion of his patrimonial fields.
Such was his first resolve; he thought again,
And his heart failed him.
                              'Isabel', said he,
Two evenings after he had heard the news,
'I have been toiling more than seventy years,
And in the open sunshine of God's love
Have we all lived, yet if these fields of ours
Should pass into a stranger's hand, I think
That I could not lie quiet in my grave.
Our lot is a hard lot; the sun itself
Has scarcely been more diligent than I,
And I have lived to be a fool at last
To my own family. An evil man
That was, and made an evil choice, if he
Were false to us; and if he were not false,
There are ten thousand to whom loss like this

Had been no sorrow. I forgive him – but
'Twere better to be dumb than to talk thus.
When I began, my purpose was to speak
Of remedies and of a cheerful hope.
Our Luke shall leave us, Isabel; the land
Shall not go from us, and it shall be free –
He shall possess it, free as is the wind
That passes over it. We have, thou knowest,
Another kinsman; he will be our friend
In this distress. He is a prosperous man,
Thriving in trade, and Luke to him shall go
And with his kinsman's help and his own thrift
He quickly will repair this loss, and then
May come again to us. If here he stay,
What can be gained?'
                                    At this the old man paused
And Isabel sat silent, for her mind
Was busy looking back into past times.
'There's Richard Bateman', thought she to herself,
'He was a parish-boy – at the church door
They made a gathering for him, shillings, pence,
And halfpennies, wherewith the neighbours bought
A basket, which they filled with pedlar's wares,
And with this basket on his arm the lad
Went up to London, found a master there,
Who out of many chose the trusty boy
To go and overlook his merchandise
Beyond the seas, where he grew wondrous rich
And left estates and monies to the poor,
And at his birthplace built a chapel, floored
With marble which he sent from foreign lands.'
   These thoughts, and many others of like sort,
Passed quickly through the mind of Isabel,
And her face brightened. The old man was glad,
And thus resumed: 'Well, Isabel, this scheme
These two days has been meat and drink to me:
Far more than we have lost is left us yet.

O blessed vision, happy child,
That art so exquisitely wild,
I think of thee with many fears
For what may be thy lot in future years.

Hartley Coleridge, David Wilkie, 1807 (Wordsworth Trust).

We have enough – I wish indeed that I
Were younger, but this hope is a good hope.
Make ready Luke's best garments; of the best
Buy for him more, and let us send him forth
Tomorrow, or the next day, or tonight –
If he could go, the boy should go tonight.'
　　Here Michael ceased, and to the fields went forth
With a light heart. The housewife for five days
Was restless morn and night, and all day long
Wrought on with her best fingers to prepare
Things needful for the journey of her son.
But Isabel was glad when Sunday came
To stop her in her work; for when she lay
By Michael's side, she for the two last nights
Heard him, how he was troubled in his sleep;
And when they rose at morning she could see
That all his hopes were gone. That day at noon
She said to Luke, while they two by themselves
Were sitting at the door: 'Thou must not go,
We have no other child but thee to lose,
None to remember – do not go away,
For if thou leave thy father he will die.'
The lad made answer with a jocund voice,
And Isabel, when she had told her fears,
Recovered heart. That evening her best fare
Did she bring forth, and all together sat
Like happy people round a Christmas fire.
　　Next morning Isabel resumed her work,
And all the ensuing week the house appeared
As cheerful as a grove in spring. At length
The expected letter from their kinsman came,
With kind assurances that he would do
His utmost for the welfare of the boy –
To which requests were added that forthwith
He might be sent to him. Ten times or more
The letter was read over; Isabel
Went forth to show it to the neighbours round;

Nor was there at that time on English land
A prouder heart than Luke's. When Isabel
Had to her house returned the old man said,
'He shall depart tomorrow.' To this word
The housewife answered, talking much of things
Which, if at such short notice he should go,
Would surely be forgotten – but at length
She gave consent, and Michael was at ease.

    Near the tumultuous brook of Greenhead Gill
In that deep valley, Michael had designed
To build a sheepfold, and before he heard
The tidings of his melancholy loss
For this same purpose he had gathered up
A heap of stones, which close to the brook-side
Lay thrown together, ready for the work.
With Luke that evening thitherward he walked,
And soon as they had reached the place he stopped,
And thus the old man spake to him: 'My son,
Tomorrow thou wilt leave me. With full heart
I look upon thee, for thou art the same
That wert a promise to me ere thy birth,
And all thy life hast been my daily joy.
I will relate to thee some little part
Of our two histories; 'twill do thee good
When thou art from me, even if I should speak
Of things thou canst not know of.
                      After thou
First camest into the world, as it befalls
To newborn infants, thou didst sleep away
Two days, and blessings from thy father's tongue
Then fell upon thee. Day by day passed on,
And still I loved thee with increasing love.
Never to living ear came sweeter sounds
Than when I heard thee by our own fireside
First uttering without words a natural tune –
When thou, a feeding babe, didst in thy joy
Sing at thy mother's breast. Month followed month,

And in the open fields my life was passed,
And in the mountains, else I think that thou
Hadst been brought up upon thy father's knees.
But we were playmates, Luke; among these hills,
As well thou knowest, in us the old and young
Have played together – nor with me didst thou
Lack any pleasure which a boy can know.'
    Luke had a manly heart; but at these words
He sobbed aloud. The old man grasped his hand,
And said, 'Nay, do not take it so – I see
That these are things of which I need not speak.
Even to the utmost have I been to thee
A kind and a good father; and herein
I but repay a gift which I myself
Received at others' hands, for though now old
Beyond the common life of man I still
Remember them who loved me in my youth.
Both of them sleep together – here they lived
As all their forefathers had done; and when
At length their time was come, they were not loth
To give their bodies to the family mould.
    I wished that thou shouldst live the life they lived;
But 'tis a long time to look back, my son,
And see so little gain from sixty years.
These fields were burdened when they came to me;
Till I was forty years of age, not more
Than half of my inheritance was mine.
I toiled and toiled; God blessed me in my work,
And till these three weeks past the land was free –
It looks as if it never should endure
Another master. Heaven forgive me, Luke,
If I judge ill for thee, but it seems good
That thou shouldst go.
               At this the old man paused,
Then pointing to the stones near which they stood,
Thus after a short silence he resumed:
'This was a work for us, and now, my son,

It is a work for me. But, lay one stone –
Here, lay it for me, Luke, with thine own hands –
I for the purpose brought thee to this place.
Nay, boy, be of good hope, we both may live
To see a better day. At eighty-four
I still am strong and stout; do thou thy part,
I will do mine. I will begin again
With many tasks that were resigned to thee;
Up to the heights, and in among the storms,
Will I without thee go again, and do
All works which I was wont to do alone
Before I knew thy face.
                              Heaven bless thee,
Thy heart these two weeks has been beating fast
With many hopes. It should be so – yes, yes,
I knew that thou couldst never have a wish
To leave me, Luke – thou hast been bound to me
Only by links of love. When thou art gone
What will be left of us? – but I forget
My purposes. Lay now the corner-stone
As I requested, and hereafter, Luke,
When thou art gone away, should evil men
Be thy companions, let this sheepfold be
Thy anchor and thy shield. Amid all fear,
And all temptation, let it be to thee
An emblem of the life thy fathers lived,
Who, being innocent, did for that cause
Bestir them in good deeds. Now, fare thee well.
When thou returnst, thou in this place wilt see
A work which is not here. A covenant
'Twill be between us – but whatever fate
Befall thee, I shall love thee to the last,
And bear thy memory with me to the grave.'
   The shepherd ended here, and Luke stooped down
And as his father had requested, laid
The first stone of the sheepfold. At the sight
The old man's grief broke from him; to his heart

He pressed his son, he kissed him and wept –
And to the house together they returned.
Next morning, as had been resolved, the boy
Began his journey; and when he had reached
The public way he put on a bold face,
And all the neighbours as he passed their doors
Came forth with wishes and with farewell prayers
That followed him till he was out of sight.

A good report did from their kinsman come
Of Luke and his well-doing; and the boy
Wrote loving letters, full of wondrous news,
Which, as the housewife phrased it, were throughout
The prettiest letters that were ever seen.
Both parents read them with rejoicing hearts.
So many months passed on, and once again
The shepherd went about his daily work
With confident and cheerful thoughts; and now
Sometimes when he could find a leisure hour
He to that valley took his way, and there
Wrought at the sheepfold. Meantime Luke began
To slacken in his duty, and at length
He in the dissolute city gave himself
To evil courses; ignominy and shame
Fell on him, so that he was driven at last
To seek a hiding-place beyond the seas.

There is a comfort in the strength of love,
'Twill make a thing endurable which else
Would break the heart – old Michael found it so.
I have conversed with more than one who well
Remember the old man, and what he was
Years after he had heard this heavy news.
His bodily frame had been from youth to age
Of an unusual strength. Among the rocks
He went, and still looked up upon the sun
And listened to the wind, and, as before,
Performed all kinds of labour for his sheep
And for the land, his small inheritance.

And to that hollow dell from time to time
Did he repair, to build the fold of which
His flock had need. 'Tis not forgotten yet
The pity which was then in every heart
For the old man, and 'tis believed by all
That many and many a day he thither went,
And never lifted up a single stone.

There by the sheepfold sometimes was he seen
Sitting alone, with that his faithful dog
(Then old) beside him, lying at his feet.
The length of full seven years from time to time
He at the building of this sheepfold wrought,
And left the work unfinished when he died.
Three years, or little more, did Isabel
Survive her husband; at her death the estate
Was sold, and went into a stranger's hand.
The cottage which was named The Evening Star
Is gone; the ploughshare has been through the ground
On which it stood. Great changes have been wrought
In all the neighbourhood; yet the oak is left
That grew beside their door, and the remains
Of the unfinished sheepfold may be seen
Beside the boisterous brook of Greenhead Gill.

To A Butterfly

Stay near me, do not take thy flight!
A little longer stay in sight –
Much reading do I find in thee,
Historian of my infancy.
Float near me, do not yet depart!
Dead times revive in thee;
Thou bringst (gay creature, as thou art)
A solemn image to my heart:
My father's family.

Oh pleasant, pleasant were the days,
The time when in our childish plays
My sister Emmeline and I
Together chased the butterfly.
A very hunter, I did rush
Upon the prey – with leaps and springs
I followed on from brake to bush –
But she, God love her, feared to brush
The dust from off its wings!

To the Cuckoo

O blithe new-comer, I have heard,
I hear thee and rejoice;
O cuckoo, shall I call thee bird,
Or but a wandering voice?

While I am lying on the grass
I hear thy restless shout;
From hill to hill it seems to pass
About and all about.

To me, no babbler with a tale
Of sunshine and of showers,
Thou tellest – cuckoo in the vale –
Of visionary hours.

Thrice welcome darling of the spring!
Even yet thou art to me
No bird, but an invisible thing,
A voice, a mystery,

The same whom in my schoolboy days,
I listened to – that cry
Which made me look a thousand ways
In bush, and tree, and sky.

To seek thee did I often rove
Through woods and on the green,
And thou wert still a hope, a love –
Still longed for, never seen.

And I can listen to thee yet,
Can lie upon the plain,
And listen till I do beget
That golden time again.

O blessed bird, the earth we pace
Again appears to be
An unsubstantial fairy place
That is fit home for thee!

The Rainbow

My heart leaps up when I behold
    A rainbow in the sky:
So was it when my life began,
So is it now I am a man,
So be it when I shall grow old,
    Or let me die!
The child is father of the man;
And I could wish my days to be
Bound each to each by natural piety.

The Cock is Crowing

The cock is crowing,
The stream is flowing,
The small birds twitter,
The lake doth glitter,
The green field sleeps in the sun.

The oldest and youngest
Are at work with the strongest,
The cattle are grazing,
Their heads never raising,
There are forty feeding like one.

Like an army defeated
The snow hath retreated,
And now doth fare ill
On top of the bare hill;
The plough-boy is whooping, anon, anon,

There's joy in the mountains,
There's life in the fountains,
Small clouds are sailing,
Blue sky prevailing –
The rain is over and gone!

To Hartley Coleridge, Six Years Old

O thou whose fancies from afar are brought,
Who of thy words dost make a mock apparel,
And fittest to unutterable thought
The breeze-like motion and the self-born carol;
Thou fairy voyager, that dost float
In such clear water, that thy boat
May rather seem
To brood on air that on an earthly stream –
Suspended in a stream as clear as sky,
Where earth and heaven do make one imagery.
O blessed vision, happy child,
That art so exquisitely wild,
I think of thee with many fears
For what may be thy lot in future years.

I thought of times when Pain might be thy guest,
Lord of thy house and hospitality;
And Grief – uneasy lover – never rest
But when she sat within the touch of thee.
Oh too industrious folly!
Oh vain and causeless melancholy!
Nature will either end thee quite,
Or, lengthening out thy season of delight,
Preserve for thee, by individual right,
A young lamb's heart among the full-grown flocks.
What hast thou to do with sorrow,
Or the injuries of tomorrow?
Thou art a dew-drop which the morn brings forth,
Not doomed to jostle with unkindly shocks
Or to be trailed along the soiling earth –
A gem that glitters while it lives,
And no forewarning gives,
But, at the touch of wrong, without a strife,
Slips in a moment out of life.

To a Butterfly

I've watched you now a full half-hour
Self-poised upon that yellow flower,
And little butterfly indeed
I know not if you sleep or feed.
How motionless! Not frozen seas
More motionless – and then,
What joy awaits you, when the breeze
Hath found you out among the trees
And calls you forth again.

This plot of orchard ground is ours
(My trees they are, my sister's flowers),
Stop here whenever you are weary
And rest as in a sanctuary.
Come often to us – fear no wrong –
Sit near us on the bough!
We'll talk of sunshine and of song,
And summer days when we were young –
Sweet childish days that were as long
As twenty days are now.

I Have Thoughts That Are Fed by the Sun

I have thoughts that are fed by the sun:
   The things which I see
   Are welcome to me,
   Welcome every one –
   I do not wish to lie
     Dead, dead,
Dead, without any company.
   Here alone on my bed
With thoughts that are fed by the sun,
And hopes that are welcome every one,
   Happy am I.

O life there is about thee
A deep delicious peace;
I would not be without thee,
   Stay, oh stay!
Yet be thou ever as now –
Sweetness and breath, with the quiet of death –
Be but thou ever as now,
   Peace, peace, peace.

The Leech-Gatherer

There was a roaring in the wind all night,
The rain came heavily and fell in floods,
But now the sun is rising calm and bright,
The birds are singing in the distant woods,
Over his own sweet voice the stock-dove broods,
The jay makes answer as the magpie chatters,
And all the air is filled with pleasant noise of waters.

All things that love the sun are out of doors,
The sky rejoices in the morning's birth,
The grass is bright with raindrops; on the moors
The hare is running races in her mirth,
And with her feet she from the plashy earth
Raises a mist which, glittering in the sun,
Runs with her all the way, wherever she doth run.

I was a traveller then upon the moor:
I saw the hare that raced about with joy,
I heard the woods and distant waters roar –
Or heard them not – as happy as a boy;
The pleasant season did my heart employ;
My old remembrances went from me wholly,
And all the ways of men, so vain and melancholy.

But, as it sometimes chanceth – from the might
Of joy in minds that can no farther go –
As high as we have mounted in delight
In our dejection do we sink as low.
To me that morning did it happen so,
And fears and fancies thick upon me came:
Dim sadness, and blind thoughts I knew not, nor could
    name.

I heard the skylark singing in the sky
And I bethought me of the playful hare:
'Even such a happy child of earth am I –
Even as these blissful creatures do I fare!
Far from the world I walk, and from all care;
But there may come another day to me
Solitude, pain of heart, distress and poverty.

My whole life I have lived in pleasant thought
As if life's business were a summer mood,
As if all needful things would come unsought
To genial faith, still rich in genial good;
But how can he expect that others should
Build for him, sow for him, and at his call
Love him, who for himself will take no heed at all?'

I thought of Chatterton, the marvellous boy,
The sleepless soul that perished in its pride;
Of him who walked in glory and in joy
Behind his plough upon the mountain's side.
By our own spirits are we deified:
We poets in our youth begin in gladness,
But thereof comes in the end despondency and madness.

Now, whether it were by peculiar grace
(A leading from above, a something given),
Yet it befell that in this lonely place
When up and down my fancy thus was driven,
And I with these untoward thoughts had striven,
I saw a man before me unawares;
The oldest man he seemed that ever wore grey hairs.

My course I stopped as soon as I espied
The old man in that naked wilderness;
Close by a pond – upon the further side –
He stood alone a minute's space, I guess.
I watched him, he continuing motionless;
To the pool's further margin then I drew,
He being all the while before me full in view.

As a huge stone is sometimes seen to lie
Couched on the bald top of an eminence
(Wonder to all who do the same espy
By what means it could thither come, and whence)
So that it seems a thing endued with sense,
Like a sea-beast crawled forth, which on a shelf
Of rock or sand reposeth, there to sun itself –

Such seemed this man, not all alive nor dead,
Nor all asleep, in his extreme old age. ·
His body was bent double, feet and head
Coming together in their pilgrimage
As if some dire constraint of pain, or rage
Of sickness, felt by him in times long past,
A more than human weight upon his frame had cast.

Himself he propped – his body, limbs, and face –
Upon a long grey staff of shaven wood;
And still, as I drew near with gentle pace,
Beside the little pond or moorish flood
Motionless as a cloud the old man stood,
That heareth not the loud winds when they call,
And moveth altogether, if it move at all.

At length – himself unsettling – he the pond
Stirred with his staff, and fixedly did look
Upon the muddy water which he conned
As if he had been reading in a book;
And now such freedom as I could I took,
And, drawing to his side, to him did say,
'This morning gives us promise of a glorious day.'

A gentle answer did the old man make
In courteous speech which forth he slowly drew,
And him with further words I thus bespake:
'What kind of work is that which you pursue? –
This is a lonesome place for one like you.'
He answered me with pleasure and surprise,
And there was, while he spoke, a fire about his eyes.

His words came feebly from a feeble chest,
Yet each in solemn order followed each
With something of a lofty utterance dressed –
Choice word and measured phrase, above the reach
Of ordinary men – a stately speech
Such as grave livers do in Scotland use,
Religious men, who give to God and man their dues.

He told me that he to this pond had come
To gather leeches, being old and poor
(Employment hazardous and wearisome!)
And he had many hardships to endure.
From pond to pond he roamed, from moor to moor,
Housing, with God's good help, by choice or chance;
And in this way he gained an honest maintenance.

The old man still stood talking at my side,
But now his voice to me was like a stream
Scarce heard – nor word from word could I divide –
And the whole body of the man did seem
Like one whom I had met with in a dream,
Or like a man from some far region sent
To give me human strength, and strong admonishment.

My former thoughts returned: the fear that kills,
The hope that is unwilling to be fed –
Cold, pain, and labour, and all fleshly ills,
And mighty poets in their misery dead.
And now, not knowing what the old man had said,
My question eagerly did I renew:
'How is it that you live, and what is it you do?'

He with a smile did then his words repeat,
And said that gathering leeches far and wide
He travelled, stirring thus about his feet
The waters of the ponds where they abide:
'Once I could meet with them on every side,
But they have dwindled long by slow decay;
Yet still I persevere, and find them where I may.'

While he was talking thus, the lonely place,
The old man's shape, and speech, all troubled me;
In my mind's eye I seemed to see him pace
About the weary moors continually,
Wandering about alone and silently.
While I these thoughts within myself pursued,
He, having made a pause, the same discourse renewed,

And soon with this he other matter blended –
Cheerfully uttered, with demeanour kind,
But stately in the main – and when he ended
I could have laughed myself to scorn to find
In that decrepit man so firm a mind.
'God', said I, 'be my help and stay secure,
I'll think of the leech-gatherer on the lonely moor!'

The Sun Has Long Been Set

The sun has long been set:
The stars are out by twos and threes;
The little birds are piping yet
Among the bushes and trees;
There's a cuckoo, and one or two thrushes,
And a noise of wind that rushes,
With a noise of water that gushes,
And the cuckoo's sovereign cry
Fills all the hollow of the sky!

Who would go 'parading'
In London, and 'masquerading',
On such a night of June,
With that beautiful soft half-moon
And all those innocent blisses –
On such a night as this is?

Sonnets of 1802

i. *I Grieved For Buonaparté*

I grieved for Buonaparté with a vain
And an unthinking grief – the vital blood
Of that man's mind, what can it be? What food
Fed his first hopes? What knowledge could *he* gain?
'Tis not in battles that from youth we train
The governor who must be wise and good,
And temper with the sternness of the brain
Thoughts motherly and meek as womanhood.
Wisdom doth live with children round her knees:
Books, leisure, perfect freedom, and the talk
Man holds with weekday man in the hourly walk
Of the mind's business. These are the degrees
By which true sway doth mount; this is the stalk
True power doth grow on – and her rights are these.

ii. *The World Is Too Much With Us*

The world is too much with us: late and soon,
Getting and spending, we lay waste our powers
(Little we see in Nature that is ours),
We have given our hearts away, a sordid boon!
This sea that bares her bosom to the moon,
The winds that will be howling at all hours
And are up-gathered now like sleeping flowers –
For this, for every thing, we are out of tune:
It moves us not. Great God, I'd rather be
A pagan suckled in a creed outworn
So might I, standing on this pleasant lea,
Have glimpses that would make me less forlorn –
Have sight of Proteus coming from the sea,
Or hear old Triton blow his wreathed horn.

iii. *It Is A Beauteous Evening*
To Caroline Wordsworth (Vallon), aged nine

It is a beauteous evening, calm and free:
The holy time is quiet as a nun
Breathless with adoration; the broad sun
Is sinking down in its tranquillity;
The gentleness of heaven is on the sea.
Listen, the mighty being is awake
And doth with his eternal motion make
A sound like thunder – everlastingly!
Dear child, dear girl, that walkest with me here,
If though appearst untouched by solemn thought
Thy nature is not therefore less divine:
Thou liest in Abraham's bosom all the year,
And worshipst at the temple's inner shrine,
God being with thee when we know it not.

iv. *To Toussaint L'Ouverture*

Toussaint – the most unhappy man of men! –
Whether the rural milkmaid by her cow
Sing in thy hearing, or thou liest now
Alone in some deep dungeon's earless den,
O miserable chieftain, where and when
Wilt thou find patience? Yet die not! Do thou
Wear rather in thy bonds a cheerful brow;
Though fallen thyself, never to rise again,
Live, and take comfort! Thou hast left behind
Powers that will work for thee – air, earth, and skies –
There's not a breathing of the common wind
That will forget thee! Thou hast great allies:
Thy friends are exultations, agonies,
And love, and man's unconquerable mind.

v. *Upon Westminster Bridge*

Earth has not anything to show more fair –
Dull would he be of soul who could pass by
A sight so touching in its majesty.
This city now doth like a garment wear
The beauty of the morning, silent, bare:
Ships, towers, domes, theatres, and temples lie
Open unto the fields and to the sky,
All bright and glittering in the smokeless air.
Never did sun more beautifully steep
In his first splendour valley, rock or hill;
Ne'er saw I, never felt, a calm so deep
(The river glideth at his own sweet will) –
Dear God, the very houses seem asleep,
And all that mighty heart is lying still!

John Milton – a model for Wordsworth's political ideals, and his great precursor among the English poets – by Jonathan Richardson, engraved 1734. 'Judge of my astonishment when, in this portrait of Milton, I saw a likeness nearly perfect, of Wordsworth. . . . In two points only was there a deviation . . . the face was a little too short and too broad, and the eyes were too large' (De Quincey, *Recollections of the Lake Poets*, 1862).

vi. *Milton, Thou Shouldst Be Living At This Hour*

Milton, thou shouldst be living at this hour,
England hath need of thee! She is a fen
Of stagnant waters! Altar, sword, and pen,
Fireside, the heroic wealth of hall and bower,
Have forfeited their ancient English dower
Of inward happiness. We are selfish men,
Oh raise us up – return to us again
And give us manners, virtue, freedom, power!
Thy soul was like a star and dwelt apart;
Thou hadst a voice whose sound was like the sea
(Pure as the naked heavens, majestic, free),
So dist thou travel on life's common way
In cheerful godliness – and yet thy heart
The lowliest duties on itself did lay.

vii. *Nuns Fret Not At Their Convent's Narrow Room*

Nuns fret not at their convent's narrow room,
And hermits are contented with their cells,
And students with their pensive citadels;
Maids at the wheel, the weaver at his loom,
Sit blithe and happy; bees that soar for bloom
High as the highest peak of Furness Fells
Will murmur by the hour in foxglove bells.
In truth, the prison unto which we doom
Ourselves, no prison is; and hence to me,
In sundry moods, 'twas pastime to be bound
Within the sonnet's scanty plot of ground –
Pleased if some souls (for such there needs must be),
Who have felt the weight of too much liberty,
Should find short solace there, as I have found.

She Was A Phantom of Delight
for Mary Wordsworth (née Hutchinson)

She was a phantom of delight
When first she gleamed upon my sight,
A lovely apparition, sent
To be a moment's ornament;
Her eyes as stars of twilight fair,
Like twilight's too her dusky hair,
But all things else about her drawn
From May-time and the cheerful dawn –
A dancing shape, an image gay,
To haunt, to startle, and waylay.

I saw her, upon nearer view,
A spirit – yet a woman too –
Her household-motions light and free,
And steps of virgin liberty;
A countenance in which did meet
Sweet records, promises as sweet;
A creature not too bright or good
For human nature's daily food,
For transient sorrows, simple wiles,
Praise, blame, love, kisses, tears, and smiles.

And now I see with eye serene
The very pulse of the machine:
A being breathing thoughtful breath,
A traveller betwixt life and death –
The reason firm, the temperate will,
Endurance, foresight, strength and skill –
A perfect woman, nobly planned,
To warn, to comfort, and command;
And yet a spirit still, and bright
With something of an angel light.

Daffodils
1804

I wandered lonely as a cloud
That floats on high o'er vales and hills,
When all at once I saw a crowd,
A host of golden daffodils –
Along the lake, beneath the trees,
Ten thousand dancing in the breeze.

The waves beside them danced, but they
Outdid the sparkling waves with glee;
A poet could not but be gay
In such a laughing company.
I gazed and gazed, but little thought
What wealth the show to me had brought:

For oft when on my couch I lie,
In vacant or in pensive mood,
They flash upon that inward eye
Which is the bliss of solitude,
And then my heart with pleasure fills
And dances with the daffodils.

Wild daffodils on Ullswater, beautifully described by Dorothy Wordsworth in a *Journal* entry, 15 April 1802, that was to become the source of her brother's most famous poem (Wordsworth Trust).

Ode to Duty

Stern daughter of the voice of God,
O Duty (if that name thou love,
Who art a light to guide, a rod
To check the erring, and reprove),
Thou who art victory and law
When empty terrors overawe;
From vain temptations dost set free,
From strife and from despair – a glorious ministry!

There are who ask not if thine eye
Be on them, who, in love and truth,
Where no misgiving is, rely
Upon the genial sense of youth.
Glad hearts, without reproach or blot,
Who do thy work and know it not,
May joy be theirs while life shall last –
And thou, if they should totter, teach them to stand fast.

Serene will be our days and bright,
And happy will our nature be,
When love is an unerring light
And joy its own security;
And blessed are they who in the main
This faith, even now, do entertain –
Live in the spirit of this creed,
Yet find that other strength, according to their need.

I, loving freedom, and untried
(No sport of every random gust,
Yet being to myself a guide),
Too blindly have reposed my trust.
Resolved that nothing e'er should press
Upon my present happiness,
I shoved unwelcome tasks away –
But thee I now would serve more strictly, if I may.

Through no disturbance of my soul,
Or strong compunction in me wrought,
I supplicate for thy control,
But in the quietness of thought.
Me this unchartered freedom tires –
I feel the weight of chance desires –
My hopes no more must change their name:
I long for a repose which ever is the same.

Yet not the less would I throughout
Still act according to the voice
Of my own wish, and feel past doubt
That my submissiveness was choice.
Not seeking in the school of pride
For 'precepts over-dignified',
Denial and restraint I prize
No farther than they breed a second will, more wise.

Stern lawgiver! – yet thou dost wear
The Godhead's most benignant grace;
Nor know we any thing so fair
As is the smile upon thy face.
Flowers laugh before thee on their beds,
And fragrance in thy footing treads;
Thou dost preserve the stars from wrong,
And the most ancient heavens through thee are fresh
    and strong.

To humbler functions, awful power,
I call thee: I myself commend
Unto thy guidance from this hour.
Oh let my weakness have an end!
Give unto me, made lowly-wise,
The spirit of self-sacrifice;
The confidence of reason give,
And in the light of truth – thy bondman – let me live!

Ode (*Intimations of Immortality*)

There was a time when meadow, grove, and stream,
The earth and every common sight
    To me did seem
    Apparelled in celestial light –
The glory and the freshness of a dream.
It is not now as it has been of yore;
    Turn wheresoe'er I may,
    By night or day,
The things which I have seen I now can see no more.

    The rainbow comes and goes,
    And lovely is the rose;
    The moon doth with delight
Look round her when the heavens are bare;
    Waters on a starry night
    Are beautiful and fair;
The sunshine is a glorious birth –
But yet I know, where'er I go,
That there hath passed away a glory from the earth.

Now, while the birds thus sing a joyous song,
    And while the young lambs bound
    As to the tabor's sound,
To me alone there came a thought of grief.
A timely utterance gave that thought relief,
    And I again am strong!
The cataracts blow their trumpets from the steep
(No more shall grief of mine the season wrong),
I hear the echoes through the mountains throng;
The winds come to me from the fields of sleep,
    And all the earth is gay;
    Land and sea
Give themselves up to jollity,
    And with the heart of May

Doth every beast keep holiday;
        Thou child of joy,
Shout round me – let me hear thy shouts, thou happy
    shepherd boy!

Ye blessed creatures I have heard the call
        Ye to each other make; I see
The heavens laugh with you in your jubilee;
        My heart is at your festival,
        My head hath its coronal,
The fullness of your bliss, I feel – I feel it all!
            Oh evil day, if I were sullen
            While the Earth herself is adorning
                This sweet May-morning,
            And the children are pulling
                On every side
            In a thousand valleys far and wide
            Fresh flowers; while the sun shines warm,
And the babe leaps up on his mother's arm.
        I hear, I hear, with joy I hear;
        But there's a tree, of many one,
A single field which I have looked upon –
Both of them speak of something that is gone.
                The pansy at my feet
                Doth the same tale repeat:
Whither is fled the visionary gleam?
Where is it gone, the glory and the dream?

Our birth is but a sleep and a forgetting:
The soul that rises with us, our life's star,
            Hath had elsewhere its setting
                And cometh from afar.
        Not in entire forgetfulness,
        And not in utter nakedness,
But trailing clouds of glory do we come
                From God who is our home.
Heaven lies about us in our infancy –

'The cataracts blow their trumpets from the steep'. *Sty Head Fall*, John Constable, September 1806 (Victoria and Albert Museum).

Shades of the prison-house begin to close
           Upon the growing boy,
But he beholds the light and whence it flows,
           He sees it in his joy.
The youth, who daily farther from the east
      Must travel, still is Nature's priest
        And by the vision splendid
        Is on his way attended;
At length the man perceives it die away
And fade into the light of common day.

Earth fills her lap with pleasures of her own:
Yearnings she hath in her own natural kind,
And even with something of a mother's mind
        And no unworthy aim
      The homely nurse doth all she can
To make her foster-child, her inmate, man
        Forget the glories he hath known,
And that imperial palace whence he came.

Behold the child among his new-born blisses,
A four years' darling of a pigmy size –
See where, mid work of his own hand, he lies,
Fretted by sallies of his mother's kisses,
With light upon him from his father's eyes!
See at his feet some little plan or chart,
Some fragment from his dream of human life
Shaped by himself with newly-learned art
        (A wedding or a festival,
        A mourning or a funeral),
          And this hath now his heart,
          And unto this he frames his song.
          Then he will fit his tongue
To dialogues of business, love or strife;
        But it will not be long
        Ere this be thrown aside,
        And with new joy and pride

The little actor cons another part,
Filling from time to time his 'humorous stage'
With all the persons down to palsied age
That life brings with her in her equipage –
          As if his whole vocation
          Were endless imitation.

Thou whose exterior semblance doth belie
          Thy soul's immensity,
Thou best philosopher, who yet dost keep
Thy heritage – thou eye among the blind
That, deaf and silent, readst the eternal deep,
Haunted for ever by the eternal mind;
          Mighty prophet, seer blest,
          On whom those truths do rest
Which we are toiling all our lives to find!
Thou over whom thy immortality
Broods like the day, a master o'er a slave –
A presence which is not to be put by –
          To whom the grave
Is but a lonely bed without the sense or sight
          Of day or the warm light,
A place of thought where we in waiting lie;
Thou little child, yet glorious in the might
Of untamed pleasures, on thy being's height
Why with such earnest pains dost thou provoke
The years to bring the inevitable yoke,
Thus blindly with thy blessedness at strife?
Full soon thy soul shall have her earthly freight,
And custom lie upon thee with a weight
Heavy as frost and deep almost as life!

          O joy that in our embers
          Is something that doth live,
          That nature yet remembers
          What was so fugitive!
The thought of our past years in me doth breed

Perpetual benedictions; not indeed
For that which is most worthy to be blessed
(Delight and liberty, the simple creed
Of childhood, whether fluttering or at rest,
With new-born hope for ever in his breast),
        Not for these I raise
        The song of thanks and praise,
    But for those obstinate questionings
    Of sense and outward things,
    Fallings from us, vanishings,
    Blank misgivings of a creature
Moving about in worlds not realised,
High instincts, before which our mortal nature
Did tremble like a guilty thing surprised –
        But for those first affections,
        Those shadowy recollections
        Which be they what they may
Are yet the fountain-light of all our day,
Are yet the master-light of all our seeing;
        Uphold us, cherish us, and make
Our noisy years seem moments in the being
Of the eternal silence – truths that wake
        To perish never,
Which neither listlessness nor mad endeavour,
        Nor man nor boy,
Nor all that is at enmity with joy,
Can utterly abolish or destroy!
        Hence in a season of calm weather,
        Though inland far we be,
Our souls have sight of that immortal sea
        Which brought us hither,
        Can in a moment travel thither
And see the children sport upon the shore,
And hear the mighty waters rolling evermore.

Then sing ye birds, sing, sing a joyous song,
        And let the young lambs bound

As to the tabor's sound!
We in thought will join your throng -
Ye that pipe and ye that play,
Ye that through your hearts today
Feel the gladness of the May!
What though the radiance which was once so bright
Be now forever taken from my sight,
Though nothing can bring back the hour
Of splendour in the grass, of glory in the flower,
We will grieve not, rather find
Strength in what remains behind:
In the primal sympathy
Which having been must ever be,
In the soothing thoughts that spring
Out of human suffering,
In the faith that looks through death,
In years that bring the philosophic mind.

And oh ye fountains, meadows, hills, and groves,
Think not of any severing of our loves;
Yet in my heart of hearts I feel your might –
I only have relinquished one delight
To live beneath your more habitual sway!
I love the brooks which down their channels fret,
Even more than when I tripped lightly as they;
The innocent brightness of a new-born day
Is lovely yet;
The clouds that gather round the setting sun
Do take a sober colouring from an eye
That hath kept watch o'er man's mortality;
Another race hath been, and other palms are won.
Thanks to the human heart by which we live –
Thanks to its tenderness, its joys, and fears –
To me the meanest flower that blows can give
Thoughts that do often lie too deep for tears.

Mystery of Man

Oh mystery of man, from what a depth
Proceed thy honours! I am lost, but see
In simple childhood something of the base
On which thy greatness stands – but this I feel,
That from thyself it is that thou must give,
Else never canst receive. The days gone by
Come back upon me from the dawn almost
Of life; the hiding-places of my power
Seem open, I approach, and then they close;
I see by glimpses now, when age comes on
May scarcely see at all; and I would give,
While yet we may, as far as words can give,
A substance and a life to what I feel:
I would enshrine the spirit of the past
For future restoration.

(*1805* xi, 328–42)

Gleams of Past Existence

As one who hangs down-bending from the side
Of a slow-moving boat upon the breast
Of a still water, solacing himself
With such discoveries as his eye can make
Beneath him in the bottom of the deeps,
Sees many beauteous sights (weeds, fishes, flowers,
Grots, pebbles, roots of trees), and fancies more,
Yet often is perplexed, and cannot part
The shadow from the substance, rocks and sky,
Mountains and clouds, from that which is indeed
The region, and the things which there abide
In their true dwelling; now is crossed by gleam
Of his own image, by a sunbeam now,
And motions that are sent he knows not whence
(Impediments that make his task more sweet) –
Such pleasant office have we long pursued
Incumbent o'er the surface of past time,
With like success.

(*1805* iv, 247–64)

Storm on Lake Coniston

It was a day
Upon the edge of autumn, fierce with storm;
The wind blew down the Vale of Coniston
Compressed as in a tunnel; from the lake
Bodies of foam took flight, and everything
Was wrought into commotion, high and low –
A roaring wind, mist, and bewildered showers,
Ten thousand thousand waves, mountains and crags,
And darkness, and the sun's tumultuous light.
Green leaves were rent in handfuls from the trees . . .
The horse and rider staggered in the blast . . .
Meanwhile, by what strange chance I cannot tell,
What combination of the wind and clouds,
A large unmutilated rainbow stood
Immoveable in heaven.

Moonlit Horse

One evening, walking in the public way,
A peasant of the valley where I dwelt
Being my chance companion, he stopped short
And pointed to an object full in view
At a small distance. 'Twas a horse, that stood
Alone upon a little breast of ground
With a clear silver moonlight sky behind.
With one leg from the ground the creature stood,
Insensible and still; breath, motion gone,
Hairs, colour, all but shape and substance gone,
Mane, ears, and tail, as lifeless as the trunk
That had no stir of breath. We paused awhile
In pleasure of the sight, and left him there,
With all his functions silently sealed up,
Like an amphibious work of Nature's hand,
A borderer dwelling betwixt life and death,
A living statue or a statued life.

(Draft for a five-book *Prelude*, 1804)

The Cave of Yordas

As when a traveller hath from open day
With torches passed into some vault of earth,
The grotto of Antiparos, or the den
Of Yordas among Craven's mountain tracts,
He looks and sees the cavern spread and grow,
Widening itself on all sides, sees, or thinks
He sees, erelong, the roof above his head,
Which instantly unsettles and recedes –
Substance and shadow, light and darkness, all
Commingled, making up a canopy
Of shapes, and forms, and tendencies to shape,
That shift and vanish, change and interchange,
Like spectres – ferment quiet and sublime,
Which, after a short space, works less and less
Till, every effort, every motion gone,
The scene before him lies in perfect view
Exposed, and lifeless as a written book.
    But let him pause awhile and look again,
And a new quickening shall succeed, at first
Beginning timidly, then creeping fast
Through all which he beholds: the senseless mass,
In its projections, wrinkles, cavities,
Through all its surface, with all colours streaming,
Like a magician's airy pageant, parts,
Unites, embodying everywhere some pressure
Or image, recognised or new, some type
Or picture of the world – forests and lakes,
Ships, rivers, towers, the warrior clad in mail,
The prancing steed, the pilgrim with his staff,
The mitred bishop and the throned king –
A spectacle to which there is no end.

Stepping Westward

'What you are stepping westward?' 'Yea.'
'Twould be a wildish destiny
If we, who thus together roam
In a strange land, and far from home,
Were in this place the guests of Chance.
Yet who would stop, or fear to advance,
Though home or shelter he had none,
With such a sky to lead him on?

The dewy ground was dark and cold;
Behind, all gloomy to behold;
And stepping westward seemed to be
A kind of heavenly destiny.
I liked the greeting – 'twas a sound
Of something without place or bound,
And seemed to give me spiritual right
To travel through that region bright.

The voice was soft, and she who spake
Was walking by her native lake;
The salutation had to me
The very sound of courtesy.
Its power was felt – and while my eye
Was fixed upon the glowing sky,
The echo of the voice enwrought
A human sweetness with the thought
Of travelling through the world that lay
Before me in my endless way.

The Solitary Reaper

Behold her, single in the field,
Yon solitary highland lass,
Reaping and singing by herself –
Stop here, or gently pass!
Alone she cuts and binds the grain,
And sings a melancholy strain:
O listen, for the vale profound
Is overflowing with the sound!

No nightingale did ever chant
So sweetly to reposing bands
Of travellers in some shady haunt
Among Arabian sands;
No sweeter voice was ever heard
In springtime from the cuckoo-bird,
Breaking the silence of the seas
Among the farthest Hebrides.

Will no one tell me what she sings?
Perhaps the plaintive numbers flow
For old, unhappy, far-off things,
And battles long ago;
Or is it some more humble lay,
Familiar matter of today –
Some natural sorrow, loss, or pain,
That has been, and may be again?

Whate'er the theme, the maiden sang
As if her song could have no ending;
I saw her singing at her work
And o'er the sickle bending;
I listened till I had my fill,
And as I mounted up the hill
The music in my heart I bore
Long after it was heard no more.

Elegiac Stanzas

Suggested by a Picture of Peele Castle in a Storm
painted by Sir George Beaumont

I was thy neighbour once, thou rugged pile,
(Four summer weeks I dwelt in sight of thee),
I saw thee every day, and all the while
Thy form was sleeping on a glassy sea.

So pure the sky, so quiet was the air –
So like, so very like, was day to day –
Whene'er I looked, thy image was still there;
It trembled, but it never passed away.

How perfect was the calm; it seemed no sleep,
No mood, which season takes away, or brings:
I could have fancied that the mighty deep
Was even the gentlest of all gentle things.

Ah, then, if mine had been the painter's hand,
To express what then I saw – and add the gleam,
The light that never was on sea or land,
The consecration, and the poet's dream –

I would have planted thee, thou hoary pile,
Amid a world how different from this,
Beside a sea that could not cease to smile,
On tranquil land, beneath a sky of bliss!

Thou shouldst have seemed a treasure-house, a mine
Of peaceful years, a chronicle of heaven –
Of all the sunbeams that did ever shine
The very sweetest had to thee been given!

A picture had it been of lasting ease,
Elysian quiet, without toil or strife;
No motion but the moving tide, a breeze,
Or merely silent Nature's breathing life.

Such, in the fond delusion of my heart,
Such picture would I at that time have made,
And seen the soul of truth in every part –
A faith, a trust, that could not be betrayed.

So once it would have been, 'tis so no more.
I have submitted to a new control –
A power is gone, which nothing can restore –
A deep distress hath humanised my soul.

Not for a moment could I now behold
A smiling sea and be what I have been!
The feeling of my loss will ne'er be old:
This, which I know, I speak with mind serene.

Then, Beaumont, friend (who would have been the friend,
If he had lived, of him whom I deplore),
This work of thine I blame not, but commend –
This sea in anger, and that dismal shore.

Oh 'tis a passionate work, yet wise and well!
Well chosen is the spirit that is here:
That hulk which labours in the deadly swell,
This rueful sky, this pageantry of fear!

And this huge castle standing here sublime,
I love to see the look with which it braves
(Cased in the unfeeling armour of old time)
The lightning, the fierce wind, and trampling waves.

Oh 'tis a passionate work, yet wise and well!
Well chosen is the spirit that is here:
That hulk which labours in the deadly swell,
This rueful sky, this pageantry of fear!

Peele Castle, Sir George Beaumont, 1806; the picture that inspired Wordsworth's *Elegiac Stanzas*, by calling to mind the drowning of his brother John in the wreck of the *Abergavenny* the previous year (Sir Francis Beaumont).

Farewell, farewell, the heart that lives alone,
Housed in a dream, at distance from the kind
(Such happiness, wherever it be known,
Is to be pitied, for 'tis surely blind);

But welcome fortitude, and patient cheer,
And frequent sights of what is to be borne –
Such sights, or worse, as are before me here:
Not without hope we suffer and we mourn.

The 'Rock of Names', carved by Wordsworth and Coleridge in 1801–2 beside Wyburn Water at the mid-point between their two homes in Grasmere and Keswick, and evoking the tender personal relationships from which their poetry emerges. Clearly discernible as well as the poets' own initials are those of Dorothy and John Wordsworth, Mary Hutchinson (whom Wordsworth married in October 1802), and her younger sister, Sara, with whom Coleridge was in love. Fragments of the Rock, saved when it was blown up by Victorian engineers at work on Thirlmere Reservoir, have now been pieced together at the Wordsworth Museum.

A Complaint: to Coleridge

There is a change, and I am poor:
Your love hath been, nor long ago,
A fountain at my fond heart's door,
Whose only business was to flow –
And flow it did, not taking heed
Of its own bounty, or my need.

What happy moments did I count!
Blessed was I then all bliss above!
Now, for this consecrated fount
Of murmuring, sparkling, living love,
What have I? (Shall I dare to tell?)
A comfortless, and hidden well.

A well of love – it may be deep
(I trust it is) and never dry –
What matter, if the waters sleep
In silence and obscurity?
Such change, and at the very door
Of my fond heart, hath made me poor.

The Solitary Doe at Bolton Abbey

The presence of this wandering doe
Fills many a damp obscure recess
With lustre of a saintly show,
And, reappearing, she no less
To the open day gives blessedness.
But say, among these holy places,
Which thus assiduously she paces,
Comes she with a votary's task,
Rite to perform, or boon to ask?
Fair pilgrim, harbours she a sense
Of sorrow or of reverence?

Can she be grieved for quire or shrine,
Crushed as if by wrath divine;
For what survives of house where God
Was worshipped, or where man abode;
For old magnificence undone,
Or for the gentler work begun
By Nature (softening and concealing,
And busy with a hand of healing);
The altar whence the cross was rent,
Now rich with mossy ornament;
The dormitory's length laid bare
Where the wild rose blossoms fair;
And sapling ash, whose place of birth
Is that lordly chamber's hearth?
　She sees a warrior carved in stone,
Among the thick weeds stretched alone –
A warrior, with his shield of pride
Cleaving humbly to his side,
And hands in resignation prest
Palm to palm on his tranquil breast.
Methinks she passes by the sight
As a common creature might –

If she be doomed to inward care,
Or service, it must lie elsewhere!
   But hers are eyes serenely bright
And on she moves, with pace how light,
Nor spares to stoop her head and taste
The dewy turf with flowers bestrown;
And in this way she fares, till at last
Beside the ridge of a grassy grave
In quietness she lays her down,
Gentle as a weary wave
Sinks, when the summer breeze hath died,
Against an anchored vessel's side;
Even so, without distress, doth she
Lie down in peace, and lovingly.
                    (*White Doe of Rylstone*)

Saint Paul's

Pressed with conflicting thoughts of love and fear
I parted from thee, friend, and took my way
Through the great city, pacing with an eye
Downcast, ear sleeping, and feet masterless,
That were sufficient guide unto themselves,
And step by step went pensively. Now, mark –
Not how my trouble was entirely hushed
(That might not be), but how by sudden gift,
Gift of imagination's holy power,
My soul in her uneasiness received
An anchor of stability.
                                    It chanced
That while I thus was pacing I raised up
My heavy eyes and instantly beheld,
Saw at a glance in that familiar spot,
A visionary scene: a length of street
Laid open in its morning quietness,
Deep, hollow, unobstructed, vacant, smooth,
And white with winter's purest white – as fair,
As fresh and spotless as he ever sheds
On field or mountain. Moving form was none,
Save here and there a shadowy passenger;
Slow, shadowy, silent, dusky, and beyond
And high above this winding length of street
(This noiseless and unpeopled avenue),
Pure, silent, solemn, beautiful, was seen
The huge majestic temple of St Paul
In awful sequestration, through a veil,
Through its own sacred veil, of falling snow.

Cloudscape New Jerusalem

                    The shepherds homeward moved
Through the dull mist, I following – when a step,
A single step, that freed me from the skirts
Of the blind vapour, opened to my view
Glory beyond all glory ever seen
By waking sense or by the dreaming soul . . .
The appearance instantaneously disclosed
Was of a mighty city – boldly say,
A wilderness of building – sinking far
And self-withdrawn into a wondrous depth,
Far sinking into splendour, without end!
Fabric it seemed of diamond and of gold,
With alabaster domes and silver spires,
And blazing terrace upon terrace high
Uplifted; here, serene pavilions bright
In avenues disposed; there, towers begirt
With battlements that on their restless fronts
Bore stars, illumination of all gems!
    By earthly Nature had the effect been wrought
Upon the dark materials of the storm,
Now pacified – on them, and on the coves
And mountain-steeps and summits, whereunto
The vapours had receded, taking there
Their station under a cerulean sky.
O, 'twas an unimaginable sight:
Clouds, mists, streams, watery rocks and emerald turf,
Clouds of all tincture, rocks and sapphire sky,
Confused, commingled, mutually inflamed,
Molten together, and composing thus
(Each lost in each) that marvellous array
Of temple, palace, citadel, and huge
Fantastic pomp of structure without name,
In fleecy folds voluminous, enwrapped.
    Right in the midst, where interspace appeared

Of open court, an object like a throne
Beneath a shining canopy of state
Stood fixed, and fixed resemblances were seen
To implements of ordinary use,
But vast in size, in substance glorified,
Such as by Hebrew prophets were beheld
In vision (forms uncouth of mightiest power,
For admiration and mysterious awe).
Below me was the earth. This little vale
Lay low beneath my feet – 'twas visible,
I saw not, but I felt that it was there –
That which I *saw* was the revealed abode
Of spirits in beatitude. My heart
Swelled in my breast: 'I have been dead', I cried
'And now I live! Oh, wherefore do I live?' –
And with that pang, I prayed to be no more.

(1814 *Excursion* ii, 858–907)

Two-Fold Image

                     Forth we went,
And down the valley on the streamlet's bank
Pursued our way, a broken company,
Mute or conversing, single or in pairs.
Thus having reached a bridge that overarched
The hasty rivulet where it lay becalmed
In a deep pool, by happy chance we saw
A two-fold image: on a grassy bank
A snow-white ram, and in the crystal flood
Another and the same! Most beautiful
On the green turf, with his imperial front
Shaggy and bold, and wreathed horns superb,
The breathing creature stood – as beautiful
Beneath him showed his shadowy counterpart.
Each had his glowing mountains, each his sky,
And each seemed centre of his own fair world:
Antipodes unconscious of each other,
Yet, in partition, with their several spheres,
Blended in perfect stillness to our sight!

             (1814 *Excursion* ix, 436–54)

Surprised by Joy
To Catharine Wordsworth, d. 1812, aged three

Surprised by joy, impatient as the wind,
I wished to share the transport – oh, with whom
But thee, long-buried in the silent tomb,
That spot which no vicissitude can find?
Love, faithful love, recalled thee to my mind –
But how could I forget thee? Through what power
Even for the least division of an hour
Have I been so beguiled as to be blind
To my most grievous loss? That thought's return
Was the worst pang that sorrow ever bore –
Save one, one only, when I stood forlorn,
Knowing my heart's best treasure was no more,
That neither present time, nor years unborn,
Could to my sight that heavenly face restore.

Daffodils
1815

I wandered lonely as a cloud
That floats on high o'er vales and hills,
When all at once I saw a crowd,
A host of golden daffodils –
Along the lake, beneath the trees,
Fluttering and dancing in the breeze.

Continuous as the stars that shine
And twinkle on the milky way,
They stretched in never-ending line
Along the margin of a bay:
Ten thousand saw I at a glance,
Tossing their heads in sprightly dance.

The waves beside them danced, but they
Outdid the sparkling waves in glee;
A poet could not but be gay
In such a jocund company.
I gazed and gazed, but little thought
What wealth the show to me had brought:

For oft when on my couch I lie,
In vacant or in pensive mood,
They flash upon that inward eye
Which is the bliss of solitude,
And then my heart with pleasure fills
And dances with the daffodils.

The River Duddon: Conclusion

I thought of thee, my partner and my guide,
As being past away. Vain sympathies –
For backward, Duddon, as I cast my eyes,
I see what was, and is, and will abide.
Still glides the stream, and shall forever glide
(The form remains, the function never dies),
While we, the brave, the mighty, and the wise –
We men, who in our morn of youth defied
The elements – must vanish. Be it so!
Enough if something from our hands have power
To live, and act, and serve the future hour;
And if, as toward the silent tomb we go,
Through love, through hope, and faith's transcendent
  dower,
We feel that we are greater than we know.

The poet aged 72. *Wordsworth on Helvellyn*, Benjamin Robert
Haydon, 1842 (National Portrait Gallery).

Airey-Force Valley

                          Not a breath of air
Ruffles the bosom of this leafy glen.
From the brook's margin, wide around, the trees
Are steadfast as the rocks; the brook itself,
Old as the hills that feed it from afar,
Doth rather deepen than disturb the calm
Where all things else are still and motionless.

And yet, even now, a little breeze (perchance
Escaped from boisterous winds that rage without)
Has entered, by the sturdy oaks unfelt –
But to its gentle touch how sensitive
Is the light ash, that, pendent from the brow
Of yon dim cave, in seeming silence makes
A soft eye-music of slow-waving boughs,
Powerful almost as vocal harmony
To stay the wanderer's steps and soothe his thoughts.

Extempore Effusion upon the Death of James Hogg

1835

When first, descending from the moorlands,
I saw the stream of Yarrow glide
Along a bare and open valley,
The Ettrick Shepherd was my guide;

When last along its banks I wandered,
Through groves that had begun to shed
Their golden leaves upon the pathways,
My steps the Border Minstrel led:

The mighty Minstrel breathes no longer,
Mid mouldering ruins low he lies,
And death upon the braes of Yarrow
Has closed the shepherd poet's eyes.

Nor has the rolling year twice measured,
From sign to sign, its steadfast course,
Since every mortal power of Coleridge
Was frozen at its marvellous source –

The rapt one, of the godlike forehead,
The heaven-eyed creature sleeps in earth;
And Lamb, the frolic and the gentle,
Has vanished from his lonely hearth.

Like clouds that rake the mountain-summits,
Or waves that own no curbing hand,
How fast has brother followed brother
From sunshine to the sunless land!

Yet I, whose lids from infant slumbers
Were earlier raised, remain to hear
A timid voice that asks in whispers,
'Who next will drop and disappear?'

Our haughty life is crowned with darkness,
Like London with its own black wreath,
On which with thee, O Crabbe, forth looking,
I gazed from Hampstead's breezy heath.

As if but yesterday departed,
Thou too art gone before – yet why,
For ripe fruit, seasonably gathered,
Should frail survivors heave a sigh?

No more of old romantic sorrows
For slaughtered youth or love-lorn maid!
With sharper grief is Yarrow smitten,
And Ettrick mourns with her their poet dead.